The Quebec Decision

The Quebec Decision

Perspectives on the Supreme Court Ruling on Secession

Edited by David Schneiderman

James Lorimer & Company Ltd., Publishers
Toronto, 1999

James Lorimer & Company Ltd. acknowledges the support of the Department of Canadian Heritage and the Ontario Arts Council in the development of writing and publishing in Canada. We acknowledge the support of the Canada Council for the Arts for our publishing program.

Cover: Bado

Canadian Cataloguing in Publication Data

Main entry under title:

The Quebec decision: perspectives on the Supreme Court ruling on secession

Includes index.
ISBN 1-55028-661-7 (bound)   ISBN 1-55028-660-9 (pbk.)

1. Secession — Quebec (Province). 2. Constitutional amendments — Canada. 3. Quebec (Province) — History — Autonomy and independence movements. 4. Self-determination, National — Quebec (Province). I. Schneiderman, David, 1958-

KE4216.35.S42Q42 1999   342.71'039   C99-930328-7
KF4483.A4Q42 1999

James Lorimer & Company Ltd., Publishers
35 Britain Street
Toronto, Ontario
M5A 1R7

Printed and bound in Canada

Contents

Acknowledgements

As this is a collaborative enterprise, there are many people to thank. Martha Jackman and Donna Greschner helped the project along in its early stages. The Centre for Constitutional Studies provided key institutional support and permitted the publication of material originally published in the Centre quarterly, *Constitutional Forum constitutionnel*. Patrick Monahan also kindly agreed to the publication of material that appeared originally in *Canada Watch*. Christine Urquhart of the Centre for Constitutional Studies provided able assistance at critical moments. And Diane Young and Ward McBurney of Lorimer succeeded in keeping this project on track with humour and understanding. All of the contributors deserve special thanks for meeting strict time lines and agreeing, in some cases, to leaving pieces of their arguments on the cutting room floor.

The following contributors have generously given permission to reprint their work: Jean Leclair, Bruce Ryder, Andrew Orkin, Joanna Birenbaum, Robert A. Young, Josée Legault, Jacques-Yvan Morin, Ted Morton, José Woehrling, John Whyte, Paul Joffe, Alan C. Cairns, Claude Ryan, and Donna Greschner.

David Schneiderman
Edmonton, Alberta
April 1999

Introduction

David Schneiderman

David Schneiderman is Executive Director, Centre for Constitutional Studies, University of Alberta

"When the country gets into trouble, the Supreme Court has been there to come to the rescue."[1] This is the view of Antonio Lamer, Chief Justice of the Supreme Court of Canada, reflecting on the Supreme Court's decision on the question of Quebec's unilateral secession. In 1996, the Supreme Court was asked its opinion on three questions: whether a unilateral declaration of independence by Quebec would offend the Canadian Constitution, whether it would be consistent with the rules of international law and, if the answers to the domestic and international law questions were inconsistent, which legal regime prevailed. To no one's real surprise, the Court ruled in August 1998 that unilateral secession was contrary to both Canadian constitutional law and public international law. But to the surprise of many, the Court went further and declared that there was a "constitutional duty" on the part of the provinces and the federal government to negotiate should the citizens of Quebec decide to pursue secession. The Court in effect laid down the rules for the break-up of the country. The decision was applauded by federalists and separatists alike. The Chief Justice had reason to feel some sense of satisfaction with the outcome.

The Quebec decision placed the Supreme Court at the centre of a political maelstrom over future relations between Quebec and the rest of Canada. The reference to the Court was one of the key elements in a series of politically calculated moves made by the Chrétien government intended to counteract both the sovereignist threat and the appearance of federalist ineptitude in the face of that threat. It may be more accurate to say that it was the Court that was in trouble and that, in this case, it managed to save itself.

But the justices of the Supreme Court of Canada recognized the importance of this constitutional moment. Rather than being mired only in a detailed reading of constitutional text and past legal rulings, the unanimous decision of the Court is more concerned with constitutional purposes and political realities. According to Supreme Court Justice John Major, the decision was written for all Canadian citizens to read, not merely for lawyers and law professors.[2] The constitutional lesson the Court delivers is that Canada is an ongoing project, that its unity is not inviolate, and that the politics of intransigence —referring to extremists on both side of the debate — have little to contribute to the constitutional challenges that lie ahead. Rather than conducting constitutional conversations from fixed and rigid positions, we are invited to continue that conversation in the full knowledge that there will be no certainty as to the outcome.

The Referendum

In order to understand why the federal government referred these questions to the Court, it is necessary to return to the 1995 Quebec referendum. In October 1995 Quebecers were asked to approve a process for the declaration of sovereignty after making an offer for political and economic partnership with the rest of Canada. All of this was set out in Bill 1, *An Act Respecting the Future of Quebec*, and the tripartite agreement reached between the Parti Québécois, Action Démocratique du Québec and Bloc Québécois. Bill 1 entitled the National Assembly unilaterally to declare Quebec sovereign one year after the referendum date, unless an earlier date was adopted by the legislature.

The one-year grace period was intended to provide Quebec and Canada with the time in which to settle a number of outstanding and controversial issues after a Yes vote, such as division of property and the debt. These "partnership" negotiations held out the hope, for some who would vote Yes, that a new federal arrangement within Canada could be secured within the one-year time period. Then Premier Jacques Parizeau should have scuttled these expectations by declaring that, once approval was secured in a referendum, the one year period would not forestall the eventual declaration of sovereignty. Instead, sovereignty would be a certainty, no matter how those partnership negotiations proceeded. Quebec would become "virtually sovereign," he declared, the day after a Yes vote.

The response of Quebec City lawyer Guy Bertrand was that the bill was a virtual constitutional *coup d'état*. Bertrand, a former

Péquiste, proceeded to court in August 1995 seeking an order that his constitutional rights were under threat by the tripartite plan for sovereignty. He also asked the court to halt the proposed referendum. Lawyers for the Premier and Attorney General of Quebec opposed the Quebec Superior Court's authority to rule on Bertrand's motion. They argued that Canadian courts had no jurisdiction to impede progress toward the sovereignty of Quebec. Justice Lesage of the Quebec Superior Court agreed with Bertrand, finding that the proposed bill flew in the face of the Constitution's amending formula and amounted to a "serious threat" to his constitutional rights and freedoms.[3] Though he agreed in substance with Bertrand's claim, Justice Lesage would not stop the impending referendum vote. Quebecers, he concluded, "wish to express themselves" on the issue.

Early on in the referendum campaign, the federalist forces expected an easy victory. But with Bloc Québécois leader Lucien Bouchard at the helm of the Yes forces, the referendum vote was transformed into a real contest. The result was startlingly close: 50.50 per cent voting No, 49.42 per cent voting Yes. An immense federalist rally in Montreal days before the vote failed to secure a stronger No victory. The Chrétien government was seen as having nearly lost the country.

So desperate was the federalist cause that, on the eve of the referendum vote, Prime Minister Chrétien committed his government to recognize Quebec as a "distinct society" and to not undertake any constitutional change that affects Quebecers without their consent — an obvious about-face for a prime minister who had vowed not to engage in any constitutional reform. Overall, the Liberal government appeared weak, unprepared and reactive. It looked as if the separatists had the upper hand. Reform Party leader Preston Manning had been calling for a harder federalist line against the sovereignist threat, and this argument seemed, in hindsight, the better tactic. It was time to pull a leaf out of the Reform playbook.

In the following year, Bertrand returned to Quebec Superior Court seeking a more permanent order from the courts. He wanted an order prohibiting the PQ government from pursuing the sovereignist option laid out in Bill 1. Lawyers for the Quebec government appeared once more to attack the jurisdiction of the court to hear the matter. Not only did the court have no supervisory role in the process leading to the accession of Quebec to sovereignty, they argued, Bertrand's case was now entirely hypothetical — the referendum vote having been lost. It was in this hearing that the federal government made its first move. Outmanoeuvred by the upstart federalist Guy Bertrand, Justice Minister Allan Rock intervened to argue that Quebec was bound by the Constitution and that the Constitution prohibited a unilateral declaration of independence. Justice Pidgeon ruled that Bertrand had meritorious arguments that should be heard by a court in full hearing. Pidgeon identified a number of issues deserving of answer.[4] These formed the basis for the three questions referred by the federal government directly to the Supreme Court of Canada.

The Reference

In his formal unveiling of the three Reference questions in September 1996, Justice Minister Rock invoked the "rule of law." According to Rock, the rule of law is "fundamental to our democratic way." Because all are bound by the law, it permits orderly, peaceful and democratic change; it does not condone revolutionary and disruptive change. The rule of law was under threat in Quebec by its government's insistence that Quebecers had the sole authority to determine their political future, unconstrained by any constitutional limitations. Invoking the rarely used power of the federal government to refer legal questions directly to the Supreme Court of Canada, Minister Rock placed before the Court three questions that would help to forestall this proposed illegal action by the National Assembly.

Though this federal initiative was couched in the language of law and order, a number of objectives could be served by referring these questions directly to the highest court. First, the federal government could be seen to be taking the initiative vis-à-vis the sovereignist threat out of the hands of the unpredictable Bertrand. It could be seen to be aggressively defending the interests of Canada — part of the so-called Plan B strategy urged by Reformers. This aggressive strategy also could serve another objective, that is, to hold in reserve a favourable Supreme Court of Canada ruling until the next Quebec referendum. At that time, the decision could be conscripted into the federalist arsenal. The Quebec electorate would be reminded that the PQ plan for sovereignty was illegal and unconstitutional. Being a law-abiding and peaceful bunch, Quebecers would not be inclined to condone illegality. The ruling would provide a hammer blow to the heads of soft sovereignists, the swing vote that could make or break a Yes result.

In the short term, however, the federal strategy yielded serious risks. The federal government would be portrayed as interfering directly in Quebec's domestic matters. It also would be accused of resorting to an institution — the Supreme Court of Canada —whose impartiality in Quebec was in some doubt. Elite opinion had charged for some time that the Court was biased against Quebec. This opinion was based on a series of constitutional disputes lost by Quebec, including a 1982 Supreme Court decision that rejected the claim that Quebec's consent was necessary to achieve constitutional change.

The Calgary Declaration

The political risks within Quebec were serious enough to prompt action on the Plan A front — that of renewed federalism. The Prime Minister actively encouraged the premiers outside of Quebec to come to an agreement on a series of principles that would recognize Quebec's distinctiveness. Recognition of Quebec's "distinct society" was sure to prompt opposition from the ranks of the Reform Party — Reform had secured its base of support opposing any special status for Quebec. Only "equality of the provinces," Reform argued, was an acceptable constitutional position.

The Premiers were justifiably fearful about opening the Pandora's box of constitutional change. After all, there had been many casualties along the constitutional highway. The result, unveiled in 1997, was the Calgary Declaration. The Declaration outlines a framework for discussion around seven principles, five of which refer expressly or implicitly to the equality of citizens and provinces. Avoiding any reference to the tarnished language of "distinct society," the recognition of Quebec refers to its "unique character," prefaced by yet another reference to equality. The Reform Party was successfully neutralized: Reform leader Preston Manning approved of the accord, basking in the increased influence Reform was having on the national unity front.

The Questions

Question 1: Under the Constitution of Canada, can the National Assembly, legislature or government of Quebec effect the secession of Quebec from Canada unilaterally?

Question 2: Does international law give the National Assembly, legislature or government of Quebec the right to effect the secession of Quebec from Canada unilaterally? In this regard, is there a right to self-determination under international law that would give the National Assembly, legislature or government of Quebec the right to effect the secession of Quebec from Canada unilaterally?

Question 3: In the event of a conflict between domestic and international law on the right of the National Assembly, legislature or government of Quebec to effect the secession of Quebec from Canada unilaterally, which would take precedence in Canada?

The federal government's strategy was to craft a series of questions confining the Court's deliberations to a few seemingly contentious matters. The anticipated answers, however, were not very much in doubt. There is no disputing the fact that, as regards the first question, the Canadian Constitution does not comprehend the unilateral secession of a province from the federation. This could not be achieved within the existing framework without, at the least, the consent of the federal government and most, if not all, of the provinces. Sovereignists argue that secession would take place outside of the existing framework and so the question of consent really is beside the point. On the second question, the Court had no specific expertise with which to answer complex questions of international law. But it seemed doubtful, on the basis of existing precedent, that international law would condone unilateral secession. The third question, from a domestic constitutional viewpoint, also was answered easily: international law does not take precedence over the Constitution. The questions either did not pose difficult constitutional issues or regarded matters beyond the expertise of the Supreme Court of Canada.

The results in the Reference, then, were pretty much a foregone conclusion. This was so much the case that the government of Quebec refused to make an appearance before the Court, condemning both the federal strategy and the Court's legitimacy as an independent arbiter in Canada's federal system. As expected, in the weeks leading up to the Court hearing, sovereignists organized to oppose the Reference. They likened the Supreme Court to the Leaning Tower of Pisa — the Court, they argued, leaned in only one direction, toward the federalist side. The hearing was further complicated by the comments of the Minister of Justice on the eve of the Reference. Anne McLellan, the new Minister, acknowledged to a *Toronto Star* reporter that unilateral secession would be "an extraordinary set of circumstances not comprehended, in our opinion, within the existing constitutional framework."[5] This confirmed, sovereignists argued, that the secession of Quebec had nothing to do with the Canadian Constitution.

With no one to argue the sovereignist side, the Court appointed an *amicus curiae,* or "friend of the court," to make those arguments.

André Joli-Coeur, a Quebec City lawyer and self-identified *souverainiste,* took up the cause with a great deal of energy, filing a series of briefs and expert opinions making what probably was the best possible case for a legal unilateral declaration of independence. Also appearing before the Court were two provinces — Saskatchewan and Manitoba — the Territories, First Nations groups, minority rights advocates and even Guy Bertrand.

The Hearing

There was no denying the significance of the hearing. It was broadcast live for four continuous days on cable. Yet, the hearing made for poor home television viewing. In most appeal hearings, the justices ask probing questions of lawyers. Here, regrettably, the justices reserved questions for only a few hours of the very last day and put them to the two main protagonists: counsel for the federal government and the *amicus curiae*. But the Court gave indications that it would resist being locked into the framework posed by the federal government's three questions. The justices were interested in a variety of post-secession scenarios that the federal government desperately wanted to avoid discussing. What will happen should negotiations break down? Must the federal government act to protect territorial interests of aboriginal peoples? What about other minority interests within the territory of Quebec? At what moment would the federal government have an obligation to remove itself from Quebec territory?

Intervenors such as Guy Bertrand and the Grand Council of the Crees had pushed the Court to consider these dimensions of secession, broader than those directly posed by the three questions. The issues were made even more complex by the fact that the aboriginal claim under international law was as strong as, or even stronger than, the Quebec claim. It was tempting, then, to applaud the Court's refusal to be manipulated in this way. The predicament the Court faced, however, was that the further it moved to the nether regions of constitutional text, the less legitimacy it had to rule on these issues.

The Decision

The opinion of the Court makes for a far better read than watching the televised hearings. In fact, it is a clever piece of business. First, the Court replied to the questions put to it by the federal government just as the Chrétien government had predicted. The unilateral secession of Quebec from the federation, the Court declared, would be contrary to the Canadian Constitution and unsupported by the principles of international law. But the Court also took the opportunity to outline a framework for the negotiated secession of Quebec from Canada. The federal government got what it wanted, then, but much more than it bargained for.

The Court made short shrift of Maître Joli-Coeur's arguments. Although silent on the question of the removal of a constituent unit from the federation, the Canadian Constitution contemplated the possibility of change, even radical change, in its amending procedures. The secession of Quebec from the federation could only be accomplished legally by using the amending procedures set out in the Constitution (para. 97). No such amendment could be accomplished unilaterally by Quebec. The strictures of the amending formula required the participation of the provinces and the federal government. The Court stopped short of identifying precisely the amending formula that would apply in this scenario — either 7 of 10 provinces representing more than 50 per cent of the population together with Parliament, or the unanimous consent of all provinces and Parliament.

On the question of international law, Maître Joli-Coeur had argued that the Court, being a court of domestic jurisdiction, had no legitimate expertise in identifying the state of international law. Moreover, the real test under international law was one of "effectivity" — establishing effective political control of the territorial boundaries of the new state. The Court, nonetheless, moved with confidence through the international law question. Assuming, but without deciding, that the citizens of the province of Quebec constituted a "people" with the right of self-determination under international law, the Court asserted that they were capable of exercising fully their self-determination within existing Canadian political structures. At best, the right to self-determination arises only (1) in situations of decolonization, (2) where a people are oppressed, or (3) where a "definable group" is denied meaningful access to government. Quebecers did not qualify under any of these international law standards (para. 138). They were not a people capable of exercising self-determination so as to remove themselves unilaterally from an existing political unit.

Domestic constitutional law was consistent with the state of international law, so there was no conflict to resolve between the two. The sovereignist argument appeared to lose on all counts. Rather than simply ending their opinion there, however, the justices also mandated that "Canada as a whole" would be obliged to negotiate with sovereignists were Quebecers clearly to prefer sovereignty over the status quo. This constitutional duty to negotiate certainly is the most surprising aspect of the decision. It does not arise clearly from the Constitution's text, our constitutional history, past practice or the practice of other federations. The Court identified a constitutional duty to negotiate should the citizens of Quebec by a "clear majority on a clear question" decide to "pursue secession" (para. 93). This duty corresponds to the right of every province and the federal government to initiate the process of constitutional change (para. 88). Were the citizens of the province of Quebec to exercise this right and embark on the process of constitutional change leading to secession, the rest of Canada could not remain indifferent. It would have to "acknowledge and respect" that expression of democratic will (para. 88). Negotiated secession would not then be inevitable — the constitutional duty would require only that good-faith negotiations be attempted.

The New Constitutional Duty

The Court surely was correct to conclude that unilateral secession is prohibited by the Canadian Constitution. It also is consistent with the constitutional framework to conclude that negotiated secession is a possibility. There really is nothing in the text of the Constitution to prohibit radical rearrangement, if not disintegration, of the Canadian federation. But there is nothing in the text about a constitutional duty to sit down at the table and take up good-faith negotiations on each and every proposed constitutional amendment.

The justices of the Supreme Court knew this, of course. This helps to explain why the newly recognized "duty" is not a legally enforceable one. The Court made clear that it would not "supervise and enforce" negotiations (para. 89). Nor would it have any role in deciding when a party to the negotiations had discharged this duty. Here, the Court admitted, it was entering the realm of politics, the outer limits of the judicial role in a constitutional democracy (para. 100). The Court was making clear that it would provide no remedy to the likes of Guy Bertrand if negotiations were not proceeding on terms that conformed to the guiding principles the Court identified.

There are four organizing principles that would guide negotiations, which correspond to four principles underlying the present constitutional framework identified by the Court: federalism, democracy, constitutionalism and the rule of law, and respect for minorities. Though not all of these principles are explicit in the text of the

Constitution, they are its "lifeblood" (para. 51). The parties would be expected to conduct negotiations "with an eye to" these constitutional principles.

If the Court relinquished any role in supervising the negotiations, who would safeguard the rights of minorities? A number of intervenors before the Supreme Court, including the Grand Council of the Crees, asked the judges to settle the question of the status of aboriginal peoples in a post-Yes Quebec. Would their consent to secession be required? Could they and their territory remain within Canada? The Court refused to follow the Crees and others along this road. The justices recognized that negotiations would be difficult and that "minority rights" — of which the Court appeared to include aboriginal rights — particularly would be vulnerable to the "give and take" of the negotiations (para. 101). In order to forestall this trading away of minority rights, the Court included their protection as one of the principles underlying the Canadian Constitution. But if there were to be "no conclusions predetermined by law on any issue" (para. 151), then presumably the Constitution could be amended to do away with certain minority rights.

The new constitutional duty to negotiate only arises, the Court tells us, if a clear majority of Quebecers responding to a clear question indicate that secession should be pursued. But again, the Court refused to play any further role in defining that standard. What constitutes a clear majority on a clear question is "subject only to political evaluation" (para. 100). There would be no judicial determination of whether these criteria ever would be satisfied. The Court would only say that the vote should be "free of ambiguity both in terms of the question asked and in terms of the support it achieves" (para. 87). These criteria would have been satisfied, sovereignists argue, by the 1995 process: the question was clear and the vote nearly satisfied the democratic threshold of "50 per cent plus one".

But the Court signalled that something more may be required to satisfy the standard of a "clear majority." The Court wrote about a "strong majority" (para. 151), a "demonstrated majority" (para. 153), an "enhanced majority" and a "substantial consensus" (para. 77). The Court also observed (in another part of the decision) that Canadians have never accepted their system as one of "simple majority rule" (para. 76). The Court having used words like "clear majority" indicates that something more than a "simple" majority is necessary to trigger the new constitutional duty to negotiate.

Péquistes never will accept, of course, that anything more than a simple majority is required to pursue secession. Nor are they likely to seek the approval of actors outside the Quebec National Assembly on the question to be asked. In other words, there likely never will be a consensus between political players in the sovereignist and federalist camps on what qualifies as a clear majority on a clear question. If so, we are back to where we began before the Reference — deadlock. In this light, the Court's ruling does not appear to have come to anyone's rescue.

The Debate Ensues

Controversy over the meaning of the Reference, nevertheless, has inserted itself into the national unity debates. In the days after the ruling, Quebec Premier Lucien Bouchard and his ministers indicated that they would enlist the duty to negotiate in the sovereignist campaign. It could help lay the foundation for the "winning conditions" Premier Bouchard required in order to hold a third sovereignty referendum. Sovereignists will hope to sway public opinion by arguing that a Yes majority will lead not to unilateral secession but to negotiations. And this could expressly be included in the question, making it more "clear." All of this is consistent with the traditional PQ position — that the rest of Canada would have to negotiate with the Quebec government after a Yes vote — and the Supreme Court now has validated that position.

Federalists, for their part, will use the decision to alert soft sovereignists to the illegitimacy of the process — terms set unilaterally, based on a simple majority vote and a vague question, will not meet the constitutional threshold for negotiations. Moreover, the duty to negotiate does not give rise to a right of secession — negotiated secession is not inevitable and stalemate is a real possibility, the Court admitted. Voting Yes would lead only to acrimony, instability and uncertainty.

Other provinces may also be able to conscript the Quebec decision into their own constitutional agendas. Shortly after the Supreme Court ruling, the Minister of Justice for Alberta, John Havelock, suggested that the province might trigger the duty to negotiate so as to require constitutional negotiations around Senate reform. Even the Reform Party of Canada got into the act, seeking an order in the Federal Court of Canada preventing the Prime Minister from filling a vacant Senate seat until Alberta residents had an opportunity to elect a "senator-in-waiting" in October 1998. Here was the so-called principle of the equality of the provinces running amok.

One further implication of the decision concerns the principles identified by the Court as underpinning the Canadian Constitution. These principles, the Court wrote, could give rise to "substantive legal obligations" which could amount to "substantive limitations" on government action (para. 54). Principles, only implied in the text, could negate constitutionally valid acts of the legislatures and Parliament. This may provide further ammunition to those who seek to use the Constitution to limit the scope of permissible government action.

The Court deftly handled the task that it was asked to complete. Answering the questions favourably for the federal government, the Court went beyond the questions asked so as to provide ammunition to sovereignists. It lent constitutional legitimacy to their argument that the rest of Canada could not ignore a Yes vote. But the sovereignists may only have been dealt blanks. The duty to negotiate only will arise where there is a clear majority responding to a clear question. Federalists have been making these arguments since before the 1995 Quebec referendum campaign. Prior to joining the Liberal cabinet, political scientist Stéphane Dion wrote that the federal government would be justified in resisting a slim Yes majority for these reasons.[6] Once the difficulties in the negotiating process with Canada emerged, support for sovereignty would be expected to slip.

For the most part, the Court refused to play out the logic of its "negotiations" scenario. The justices rightly acknowledged, however, that the conduct of the parties during the negotiation stage would have implications for recognition in the international arena. A government failing to undertake good-faith negotiations guided by the four constitutional principles would undermine its claim to legitimacy and its standing in the international community (para. 103). But the Court avoided the obvious question of what would happen if negotiations failed. The consent of some or all the provinces and the federal government is necessary to accomplish a lawful act of secession. Yet the word "consent" can hardly be found in the Court's opinion. It may have been wise to avoid a detailed discussion of the negotiations scenario. But Canadians should be under no illusion that the Court's opinion in the Secession Reference — or a reliance on the "rule of law" — can somehow forestall the chaos that would be likely to ensue after a Yes vote.

The contributions of the authors in this collection help us to unpack these multiple layers of the Supreme Court's decision. The first few essays explore the arguments made by major parties to the Reference: the federal government, the *amicus curiae,* and aboriginal peoples. The key texts of the politicians, reacting to the decision, follow. The remainder of the essays explore both the terms of the judgement and its implications for Canadian constitutional politics. The selection of essays is intended to be pluralistic: the authors reflect a variety of viewpoints and take up differing perspectives on the decision. Sovereignists and federalists in both Quebec and the rest of Canada, views both favourable and critical of the decision, are included. The power relations and power vacuums between Quebec and rest of Canada are a recurring theme in these essays.

Collectively, the essays reflect the vibrancy of constitutional debate in Canada. If it is true that Canadians are tired of talking about the Constitution, the Quebec decision should help rouse us out of our slumber. For the decision invites us to reflect anew on the ability of citizens to continue remaking this country called Canada.

The Supreme Court Decision

Reference Re the Secession of Quebec

Supreme Court of Canada: Lamer, C. J. C., L'Heureux-Dubé, Gonthier, Cory, McLachlin, Iacobucci, Major, Bastarache and Binnie, J. J.

Heard: February 16, 17, 18 and 19, 1998
Judgment rendered: August 20, 1998

REFERENCE by the Governor in Council, pursuant to s. 53 of the *Supreme Court Act*, concerning the secession of Quebec from Canada.

L. Yves Fortier, Q.C., Pierre Bienvenu, Warren J. Newman, Jean-Marc Aubry, Q.C., and *Mary Dawson, Q.C.,* for the Attorney General of Canada.

André Joli-Coeur, Michel Paradis, Louis Masson, André Binette, Clément Samson, Martin Bédard and *Martin St-Amant,* for the *amicus curiae.*

Donna J. Miller, Q.C., and *Deborah L. Carlson,* for the intervener the Attorney General of Manitoba.

Graeme G. Mitchell and *John D. Whyte, Q.C.,* for the intervener the Attorney General for Saskatchewan.

Bernard W. Funston, for the intervener the Minister of Justice of the Northwest Territories.

Stuart J. Whitley, Q.C., and *Howard L. Kushner,* for the intervener the Minister of Justice for the Government of the Yukon Territory.

Agnes Laporte and *Richard Gaudreau,* for the intervener Kitigan Zibi Anishinabeg.

Claude-Armand Sheppard, Paul Joffe and *Andrew Orkin,* for the intervener the Grand Council of the Crees (Eeyou Estchee).

Peter W. Hutchins and *Carol Hilling,* for the intervener the Makivik Corporation.

Michael Sherry, for the intervener the Chiefs of Ontario.

Raj Anand and *M. Kate Stephenson*, for the intervener the Minority Advocacy and Rights Council.

Mary Eberts and *Anne Bayefsky*, for the intervener the *Ad Hoc* Committee of Canadian Women on the Constitution.

Guy Bertrand and *Patrick Monahan*, for the intervener Guy Bertrand.

Stephen A. Scott, for the interveners Roopnarine Singh, Keith Owen Henderson, Claude Leclerc, Kenneth O'Donnell and Van Hoven Petteway.

Vincent Pouliot, on his own behalf.

By The Court —

I. Introduction

[1] This Reference requires us to consider momentous questions that go to the heart of our system of constitutional government. The observation we made more than a decade ago in *Reference re Manitoba Language Rights*, [1985] 1 S.C.R. 721 (*Manitoba Language Rights Reference*), at p. 728, applies with equal force here: as in that case, the present one "combines legal and constitutional questions of the utmost subtlety and complexity with political questions of great sensitivity". In our view, it is not possible to answer the questions that have been put to us without a consideration of a number of underlying principles. An exploration of the meaning and nature of these underlying principles is not merely of academic interest. On the contrary, such an exploration is of immense practical utility. Only once those underlying principles have been examined and delineated may a considered response to the questions we are required to answer emerge.

[2] The questions posed by the Governor in Council by way of Order in Council P.C. 1996-1497, dated September 30, 1996, read as follows:

1. Under the Constitution of Canada, can the National Assembly, legislature or government of Quebec effect the secession of Quebec from Canada unilaterally?

2. Does international law give the National Assembly, legislature or government of Quebec the right to effect the secession of Quebec from Canada unilaterally? In this regard, is there a

right to self-determination under international law that would give the National Assembly, legislature or government of Quebec the right to effect the secession of Quebec from Canada unilaterally?

3. In the event of a conflict between domestic and international law on the right of the National Assembly, legislature or government of Quebec to effect the secession of Quebec from Canada unilaterally, which would take precedence in Canada?

[3] Before turning to Question 1, as a preliminary matter, it is necessary to deal with the issues raised with regard to this Court's reference jurisdiction.

II. The Preliminary Objections to the Court's Reference Jurisdiction

[4] The *amicus curiae* argued that s. 101 of the *Constitution Act, 1867* does not give Parliament the authority to grant this Court the jurisdiction provided for in s. 53 of the *Supreme Court Act*, R.S.C., 1985, c. S-26. Alternatively, it is submitted that even if Parliament were entitled to enact s. 53 of the *Supreme Court Act*, the scope of that section should be interpreted to exclude the kinds of questions the Governor in Council has submitted in this Reference. In particular, it is contended that this Court cannot answer Question 2, since it is a question of "pure" international law over which this Court has no jurisdiction. Finally, even if this Court's reference jurisdiction is constitutionally valid, and even if the questions are within the purview of s. 53 of the *Supreme Court Act*, it is argued that the three questions referred to the Court are speculative, of a political nature, and, in any event, are not ripe for judicial decision, and therefore are not justiciable.

[5] Notwithstanding certain formal objections by the Attorney General of Canada, it is our view that the *amicus curiae* was within his rights to make the preliminary objections, and that we should deal with them.

A. The Constitutional Validity of Section 53 of the Supreme Court Act

[6] In *Re References by Governor-General in Council* (1910), 43 S.C.R. 536, affirmed on appeal to the Privy Council, [1912] A.C. 571 (*sub nom. Attorney-General for Ontario v. Attorney-General for*

Canada), the constitutionality of this Court's special jurisdiction was twice upheld. The Court is asked to revisit these decisions. In light of the significant changes in the role of this Court since 1912, and the very important issues raised in this Reference, it is appropriate to reconsider briefly the constitutional validity of the Court's reference jurisdiction.

[7] Section 3 of the *Supreme Court Act* establishes this Court both as a "general court of appeal" for Canada and as an "additional court for the better administration of the laws of Canada". These two roles reflect the two heads of power enumerated in s. 101 of the *Constitution Act, 1867*. However, the "laws of Canada" referred to in s. 101 consist only of *federal law* and statute: see *Quebec North Shore Paper Co. v. Canadian Pacific Ltd.*, [1977] 2 S.C.R. 1054, at pp. 1065-66. As a result, the phrase "additional courts" contained in s. 101 is an insufficient basis upon which to ground the special jurisdiction established in s. 53 of the *Supreme Court Act*, which clearly exceeds a consideration of federal law alone (see, e.g., s. 53(2)). Section 53 must therefore be taken as enacted pursuant to Parliament's power to create a "general court of appeal" for Canada.

[8] Section 53 of the *Supreme Court Act* is *intra vires* Parliament's power under s. 101 if, in "pith and substance", it is legislation in relation to the constitution or organization of a "general court of appeal". Section 53 is defined by two leading characteristics — it establishes an original jurisdiction in this Court and imposes a duty on the Court to render advisory opinions. Section 53 is therefore constitutionally valid only if (1) a "general court of appeal" may properly exercise an original jurisdiction; and (2) a "general court of appeal" may properly undertake other legal functions, such as the rendering of advisory opinions.

(1) May a Court of Appeal Exercise an Original Jurisdiction?

[9] The words "general court of appeal" in s. 101 denote the status of the Court within the national court structure and should not be taken as a restrictive definition of the Court's functions. In most instances, this Court acts as the exclusive ultimate appellate court in the country, and, as such, is properly constituted as the "general court of appeal" for Canada. Moreover, it is clear that an appellate court can receive, on an exceptional basis, original jurisdiction not incompatible with its appellate jurisdiction.

[10] The English Court of Appeal, the U.S. Supreme Court and certain courts of appeal in Canada exercise an original jurisdiction

in addition to their appellate functions. See *De Demko v. Home Secretary*, [1959] A.C. 654 (H.L.), at p. 660; *Re Forest and Registrar of Court of Appeal of Manitoba* (1977), 77 D.L.R. (3d) 445 (Man. C.A.), at p. 453); U.S. Constitution, art. III, § 2. Although these courts are not constituted under a head of power similar to s. 101, they certainly provide examples which suggest that there is nothing inherently self-contradictory about an appellate court exercising original jurisdiction on an exceptional basis.

[11] It is also argued that this Court's original jurisdiction is unconstitutional because it conflicts with the original jurisdiction of the provincial superior courts and usurps the normal appellate process. However, Parliament's power to establish a general court of appeal pursuant to s. 101 is plenary, and takes priority over the province's power to control the administration of justice in s. 92(14). See *Attorney-General for Ontario v. Attorney-General for Canada*, [1947] A.C. 127 (P.C.). Thus, even if it could be said that there is any conflict between this Court's reference jurisdiction and the original jurisdiction of the provincial superior courts, any such conflict must be resolved in favour of Parliament's exercise of its plenary power to establish a "general court of appeal" provided, as discussed below, advisory functions are not to be considered inconsistent with the functions of a general court of appeal.

(2) May a Court of Appeal Undertake Advisory Functions?

[12] The *amicus curiae* submits that

> [translation] [e]ither this constitutional power [to give the highest court in the federation jurisdiction to give advisory opinions] is expressly provided for by the Constitution, as is the case in India (*Constitution of India*, art. 143), *or it is not provided for therein and so it simply does not exist.* This is what the Supreme Court of the United States has held. [Emphasis added.]

[13] However, the U.S. Supreme Court did not conclude that it was unable to render advisory opinions because no such *express power* was included in the U.S. Constitution. Quite the contrary, it based this conclusion on the *express limitation* in art. III, § 2 restricting federal court jurisdiction to actual "cases" or "controversies". See, e.g., *Muskrat v. United States*, 219 U.S. 346 (1911), at p. 362. This section reflects the strict separation of powers in the American

federal constitutional arrangement. Where the "case or controversy" limitation is missing from their respective state constitutions, some American state courts *do* undertake advisory functions (e.g., in at least two states — Alabama and Delaware — advisory opinions are authorized, in certain circumstances, by statute: see Ala. Code 1975 § 12-2-10; Del. Code Ann. tit. 10, § 141 (1996 Supp.)).

[14] In addition, the judicial systems in several European countries (such as Germany, France, Italy, Spain, Portugal and Belgium) include courts dedicated to the review of constitutional claims; these tribunals do not require a concrete dispute involving individual rights to examine the constitutionality of a new law — an "abstract or objective question" is sufficient. See L. Favoreu, "American and European Models of Constitutional Justice", in D. S. Clark, ed., *Comparative and Private International Law: Essays in Honor of John Henry Merryman on His Seventieth Birthday* (1990), 105, at p. 113. The European Court of Justice, the European Court of Human Rights, and the Inter-American Court of Human Rights also all enjoy explicit grants of jurisdiction to render advisory opinions. See *Treaty establishing the European Community*, Art. 228(6); Protocol No. 2 of the *Convention for the Protection of Human Rights and Fundamental Freedoms*, Europ. T.S. No. 5, p. 36; *Statute of the Inter-American Court of Human Rights*, Art. 2. There is no plausible basis on which to conclude that a court is, by its nature, inherently precluded from undertaking another legal function in tandem with its judicial duties.

[15] Moreover, the Canadian Constitution does not insist on a strict separation of powers. Parliament and the provincial legislatures may properly confer other legal functions on the courts, and may confer certain judicial functions on bodies that are not courts. The exception to this rule relates only to s. 96 courts. Thus, even though the rendering of advisory opinions is quite clearly done outside the framework of adversarial litigation, and such opinions are traditionally obtained by the executive from the law officers of the Crown, there is no constitutional bar to this Court's receipt of jurisdiction to undertake such an advisory role. The legislative grant of reference jurisdiction found in s. 53 of the *Supreme Court Act* is therefore constitutionally valid.

B. The Court's Jurisdiction Under Section 53

[16] Section 53 provides in its relevant parts as follows:

53. (1) The Governor in Council may refer to the Court for hearing and consideration important questions of law or fact concerning

(a) the interpretation of the *Constitution Acts*;

...

(d) the powers of the Parliament of Canada, or of the legislatures of the provinces, or of the respective governments thereof, whether or not the particular power in question has been or is proposed to be exercised.

(2) The Governor in Council may refer to the Court for hearing and consideration important questions of law or fact concerning any matter, whether or not in the opinion of the Court *ejusdem generis* with the enumerations contained in subsection (1), with reference to which the Governor in Council sees fit to submit any such question.

(3) Any question concerning any of the matters mentioned in subsections (1) and (2), and referred to the Court by the Governor in Council, shall be conclusively deemed to be an important question.

[17] It is argued that even if Parliament were entitled to enact s. 53 of the *Supreme Court Act*, the questions submitted by the Governor in Council fall outside the scope of that section.

[18] This submission cannot be accepted. Question 1 is directed, at least in part, to the interpretation of the *Constitution Acts*, which are referred to in s. 53(1)(a). Both Question 1 and Question 2 fall within s. 53(1)(d), since they relate to the powers of the legislature or government of a Canadian province. Finally, all three questions are clearly "important questions of law or fact concerning any matter" so that they must come within s. 53(2).

[19] However, the *amicus curiae* has also raised some specific concerns regarding this Court's jurisdiction to answer Question 2. The question, on its face, falls within the scope of s. 53, but the concern is a more general one with respect to the jurisdiction of this Court, as a domestic tribunal, to answer what is described as a question of "pure" international law.

[20] The first contention is that in answering Question 2, the Court would be exceeding its jurisdiction by purporting to act as an international tribunal. The simple answer to this submission is that this Court would not, in providing an advisory opinion in the context of a reference, be purporting to "act as" or substitute itself for an international tribunal. In accordance with well accepted principles of international law, this Court's answer to Question 2 would not purport to bind any other state or international tribunal that might subsequently consider a similar question. The Court nevertheless has jurisdiction to provide an advisory opinion to the Governor in Council in its capacity as a national court on legal questions touching and concerning the future of the Canadian federation.

[21] Second, there is a concern that Question 2 is beyond the competence of this Court, as a domestic court, because it requires the Court to look at international law rather than domestic law.

[22] This concern is groundless. In a number of previous cases, it has been necessary for this Court to look to international law to determine the rights or obligations of some actor within the Canadian legal system. For example, in *Reference re Powers to Levy Rates on Foreign Legations and High Commissioners' Residences*, [1943] S.C.R. 208, the Court was required to determine whether, taking into account the principles of international law with respect to diplomatic immunity, a municipal council had the power to levy rates on certain properties owned by foreign governments. In two subsequent references, this Court used international law to determine whether the federal government or a province possessed proprietary rights in certain portions of the territorial sea and continental shelf (*Reference re Ownership of Offshore Mineral Rights of British Columbia*, [1967] S.C.R. 792; *Reference re Newfoundland Continental Shelf*, [1984] 1 S.C.R. 86).

[23] More importantly, Question 2 of this Reference does not ask an abstract question of "pure" international law but seeks to determine the legal rights and obligations of the National Assembly, legislature or government of Quebec, institutions that clearly exist as part of the Canadian legal order. As will be seen, the *amicus curiae* himself submitted that the success of any initiative on the part of Quebec to secede from the Canadian federation would be governed by international law. In these circumstances, a consideration of international law in the context of this Reference about the legal aspects of the unilateral secession of Quebec is not only permissible but unavoidable.

C. *Justiciability*

[24] It is submitted that even if the Court has jurisdiction over the questions referred, the questions themselves are not justiciable. Three main arguments are raised in this regard:

(1) the questions are not justiciable because they are too "theoretical" or speculative;

(2) the questions are not justiciable because they are political in nature;

(3) the questions are not yet ripe for judicial consideration.

[25] In the context of a reference, the Court, rather than acting in its traditional adjudicative function, is acting in an advisory capacity. The very fact that the Court may be asked hypothetical questions in a reference, such as the constitutionality of proposed legislation, engages the Court in an exercise it would never entertain in the context of litigation. No matter how closely the procedure on a reference may mirror the litigation process, a reference does not engage the Court in a disposition of rights. For the same reason, the Court may deal on a reference with issues that might otherwise be considered not yet "ripe" for decision.

[26] Though a reference differs from the Court's usual adjudicative function, the Court should not, even in the context of a reference, entertain questions that would be inappropriate to answer. However, given the very different nature of a reference, the question of the appropriateness of answering a question should not focus on whether the dispute is formally adversarial or whether it disposes of cognizable rights. Rather, it should consider whether the dispute is appropriately addressed by a court of law. As we stated in *Reference re Canada Assistance Plan (B.C.)*, [1991] 2 S.C.R. 525, at p. 545:

> While there may be many reasons why a question is non-justiciable, in this appeal the Attorney General of Canada submitted that to answer the questions would draw the Court into a political controversy and involve it in the legislative process. In exercising its discretion whether to determine a matter that is alleged to be non-justiciable, *the Court's primary concern is to retain its proper role within the constitutional framework of our democratic form of government.* ... In considering its appropri-

ate role the Court must determine whether the question is purely political in nature and should, therefore, be determined in another forum or *whether it has a sufficient legal component to warrant the intervention of the judicial branch.* [Emphasis added.]

Thus the circumstances in which the Court may decline to answer a reference question on the basis of "non-justiciability" include:

(i) if to do so would take the Court beyond its own assessment of its proper role in the constitutional framework of our democratic form of government or

(ii) if the Court could not give an answer that lies within its area of expertise: the interpretation of law.

[27] As to the "proper role" of the Court, it is important to underline, contrary to the submission of the *amicus curiae*, that the questions posed in this Reference do not ask the Court to usurp any democratic decision that the people of Quebec may be called upon to make. The questions posed by the Governor in Council, as we interpret them, are strictly limited to aspects of the legal framework in which that democratic decision is to be taken. The attempted analogy to the U.S. "political questions" doctrine therefore has no application. The legal framework having been clarified, it will be for the population of Quebec, acting through the political process, to decide whether or not to pursue secession. As will be seen, the legal framework involves the rights and obligations of Canadians who live outside the province of Quebec, as well as those who live within Quebec.

[28] As to the "legal" nature of the questions posed, if the Court is of the opinion that it is being asked a question with a significant extralegal component, it may interpret the question so as to answer only its legal aspects; if this is not possible, the Court may decline to answer the question. In the present Reference the questions may clearly be interpreted as directed to legal issues, and, so interpreted, the Court is in a position to answer them.

[29] Finally, we turn to the proposition that even though the questions referred to us are justiciable in the "reference" sense, the Court must still determine whether it should exercise its discretion to refuse to answer the questions on a pragmatic basis.

[30] Generally, the instances in which the Court has exercised its discretion to refuse to answer a reference question that is otherwise justiciable can be broadly divided into two categories. First, where the question is too imprecise or ambiguous to permit a complete or accurate answer: see, e.g., *McEvoy v. Attorney General for New Brunswick*, [1983] 1 S.C.R. 704; *Reference re Waters and Water-Powers*, [1929] S.C.R. 200; *Reference re Goods and Services Tax*, [1992] 2 S.C.R. 445; *Reference re Remuneration of Judges of the Provincial Court of Prince Edward Island*, [1997] 3 S.C.R. 3 (*Provincial Judges Reference*), at para. 256. Second, where the parties have not provided sufficient information to allow the Court to provide a complete or accurate answer: see, e.g., *Reference re Education System in Montreal*, [1926] S.C.R. 246; *Reference re Authority of Parliament in Relation to the Upper House*, [1980] 1 S.C.R. 54 (*Senate Reference*); *Provincial Judges Reference*, at para. 257.

[31] There is no doubt that the questions posed in this Reference raise difficult issues and are susceptible to varying interpretations. However, rather than refuse to answer at all, the Court is guided by the approach advocated by the majority on the "conventions" issue in *Reference re Resolution to Amend the Constitution*, [1981] 1 S.C.R. 753 (*Patriation Reference*), at pp. 875-76:

> If the questions are thought to be ambiguous, this Court should not, in a constitutional reference, be in a worse position than that of a witness in a trial and feel compelled simply to answer yes or no. Should it find that a question might be misleading, or should it simply avoid the risk of misunderstanding, the Court is free either to interpret the question ... or it may qualify both the question and the answer ...

The Reference questions raise issues of fundamental public importance. It cannot be said that the questions are too imprecise or ambiguous to permit a proper legal answer. Nor can it be said that the Court has been provided with insufficient information regarding the present context in which the questions arise. Thus, the Court is duty bound in the circumstances to provide its answers.

III. Reference Questions

A. Question 1

Under the Constitution of Canada, can the National Assembly, legislature or government of Quebec effect the secession of Quebec from Canada unilaterally?

(1) Introduction

[32] As we confirmed in *Reference re Objection by Quebec to a Resolution to Amend the Constitution*, [1982] 2 S.C.R. 793, at p. 806, "The *Constitution Act, 1982* is now in force. Its legality is neither challenged nor assailable." The "Constitution of Canada" certainly includes the constitutional texts enumerated in s. 52(2) of the *Constitution Act, 1982*. Although these texts have a primary place in determining constitutional rules, they are not exhaustive. The Constitution also "embraces unwritten, as well as written rules", as we recently observed in the *Provincial Judges Reference, supra*, at para. 92. Finally, as was said in the *Patriation Reference, supra*, at p. 874, the Constitution of Canada includes

> the global system of rules and principles which govern the exercise of constitutional authority in the whole and in every part of the Canadian state.

These supporting principles and rules, which include constitutional conventions and the workings of Parliament, are a necessary part of our Constitution because problems or situations may arise which are not expressly dealt with by the text of the Constitution. In order to endure over time, a constitution must contain a comprehensive set of rules and principles which are capable of providing an exhaustive legal framework for our system of government. Such principles and rules emerge from an understanding of the constitutional text itself, the historical context, and previous judicial interpretations of constitutional meaning. In our view, there are four fundamental and organizing principles of the Constitution which are relevant to addressing the question before us (although this enumeration is by no means exhaustive): federalism; democracy; constitutionalism and the rule of law; and respect for minorities. The foundation and substance of these principles are addressed in the following paragraphs. We will then turn to their specific application to the first reference question before us.

(2) Historical Context: The Significance of Confederation

[33] In our constitutional tradition, legality and legitimacy are linked. The precise nature of this link will be discussed below. However, at this stage, we wish to emphasize only that our constitutional history demonstrates that our governing institutions have adapted and changed to reflect changing social and political values. This has generally been accomplished by methods that have ensured continuity, stability and legal order.

[34] Because this Reference deals with questions fundamental to the nature of Canada, it should not be surprising that it is necessary to review the context in which the Canadian union has evolved. To this end, we will briefly describe the legal evolution of the Constitution and the foundational principles governing constitutional amendments. Our purpose is not to be exhaustive, but to highlight the features most relevant in the context of this Reference.

[35] Confederation was an initiative of elected representatives of the people then living in the colonies scattered across part of what is now Canada. It was not initiated by Imperial *fiat*. In March 1864, a select committee of the Legislative Assembly of the Province of Canada, chaired by George Brown, began to explore prospects for constitutional reform. The committee's report, released in June 1864, recommended that a federal union encompassing Canada East and Canada West, and perhaps the other British North American colonies, be pursued. A group of Reformers from Canada West, led by Brown, joined with Etienne P. Taché and John A. Macdonald in a coalition government for the purpose of engaging in constitutional reform along the lines of the federal model proposed by the committee's report.

[36] An opening to pursue federal union soon arose. The leaders of the maritime colonies had planned to meet at Charlottetown in the fall to discuss the perennial topic of maritime union. The Province of Canada secured invitations to send a Canadian delegation. On September 1, 1864, 23 delegates (five from New Brunswick, five from Nova Scotia, five from Prince Edward Island, and eight from the Province of Canada) met in Charlottetown. After five days of discussion, the delegates reached agreement on a plan for federal union.

[37] The salient aspects of the agreement may be briefly outlined. There was to be a federal union featuring a bicameral central legislature. Representation in the Lower House was to be based on population, whereas in the Upper House it was to be based on regional

equality, the regions comprising Canada East, Canada West and the Maritimes. The significance of the adoption of a federal form of government cannot be exaggerated. Without it, neither the agreement of the delegates from Canada East nor that of the delegates from the maritime colonies could have been obtained.

[38] Several matters remained to be resolved, and so the Charlottetown delegates agreed to meet again at Quebec in October, and to invite Newfoundland to send a delegation to join them. The Quebec Conference began on October 10, 1864. Thirty-three delegates (two from Newfoundland, seven from New Brunswick, five from Nova Scotia, seven from Prince Edward Island, and twelve from the Province of Canada) met over a two and a half week period. Precise consideration of each aspect of the federal structure preoccupied the political agenda. The delegates approved 72 resolutions, addressing almost all of what subsequently made its way into the final text of the *Constitution Act, 1867*. These included guarantees to protect French language and culture, both directly (by making French an official language in Quebec and Canada as a whole) and indirectly (by allocating jurisdiction over education and "Property and Civil Rights in the Province" to the provinces). The protection of minorities was thus reaffirmed.

[39] Legally, there remained only the requirement to have the Quebec Resolutions put into proper form and passed by the Imperial Parliament in London. However, politically, it was thought that more was required. Indeed, Resolution 70 provided that "The Sanction of the Imperial and *Local Parliaments* shall be sought for the Union of the Provinces on the principles adopted by the Conference." (Cited in J. Pope, ed., *Confederation: Being a Series of Hitherto Unpublished Documents Bearing on the British North America Act* (1895), at p. 52 (emphasis added).)

[40] Confirmation of the Quebec Resolutions was achieved more smoothly in central Canada than in the Maritimes. In February and March 1865, the Quebec Resolutions were the subject of almost six weeks of sustained debate in both houses of the Canadian legislature. The Canadian Legislative Assembly approved the Quebec Resolutions in March 1865 with the support of a majority of members from both Canada East and Canada West. The governments of both Prince Edward Island and Newfoundland chose, in accordance with popular sentiment in both colonies, not to accede to the Quebec Resolutions. In New Brunswick, a general election was required before Premier Tilley's pro-Confederation party prevailed. In Nova Scotia, Premier Tupper

ultimately obtained a resolution from the House of Assembly favouring Confederation.

[41] Sixteen delegates (five from New Brunswick, five from Nova Scotia, and six from the Province of Canada) met in London in December 1866 to finalize the plan for Confederation. To this end, they agreed to some slight modifications and additions to the Quebec Resolutions. Minor changes were made to the distribution of powers, provision was made for the appointment of extra senators in the event of a deadlock between the House of Commons and the Senate, and certain religious minorities were given the right to appeal to the federal government where their denominational school rights were adversely affected by provincial legislation. The British North America Bill was drafted after the London Conference with the assistance of the Colonial Office, and was introduced into the House of Lords in February 1867. The Act passed third reading in the House of Commons on March 8, received royal assent on March 29, and was proclaimed on July 1, 1867. The Dominion of Canada thus became a reality.

[42] There was an early attempt at secession. In the first Dominion election in September 1867, Premier Tupper's forces were decimated: members opposed to Confederation won 18 of Nova Scotia's 19 federal seats, and in the simultaneous provincial election, 36 of the 38 seats in the provincial legislature. Newly-elected Premier Joseph Howe led a delegation to the Imperial Parliament in London in an effort to undo the new constitutional arrangements, but it was too late. The Colonial Office rejected Premier Howe's plea to permit Nova Scotia to withdraw from Confederation. As the Colonial Secretary wrote in 1868:

The neighbouring province of New Brunswick has entered into the union in reliance on having with it the sister province of Nova Scotia; and vast obligations, political and commercial, have already been contracted on the faith of a measure so long discussed and so solemnly adopted. ... I trust that the Assembly and the people of Nova Scotia will not be surprised that the Queen's government feel that they would not be warranted in advising the reversal of a great measure of state, attended by so many extensive consequences already in operation.

(Quoted in H. Wade MacLauchlan, "Accounting for Democracy and the Rule of Law in the Quebec Secession Reference" (1997), 76 Can. Bar Rev. 155, at p. 168.)

The interdependence characterized by "vast obligations, political and commercial", referred to by the Colonial Secretary in 1868, has, of course, multiplied immeasurably in the last 130 years.

[43] Federalism was a legal response to the underlying political and cultural realities that existed at Confederation and continue to exist today. At Confederation, political leaders told their respective communities that the Canadian union would be able to reconcile diversity with unity. It is pertinent, in the context of the present Reference, to mention the words of George-Etienne Cartier (cited in the *Parliamentary Debates on the subject of the Confederation* (1865), at p. 60):

[translation] Now, when we [are] united together, if union is attained, we [shall] form a political nationality with which neither the national origin, nor the religion of any individual, [will] interfere. It was lamented by some that we had this diversity of races, and hopes were expressed that this distinctive feature would cease. The idea of unity of races [is] utopian — it [is] impossible. Distinctions of this kind [will] always exist. Dissimilarity, in fact, appear[s] to be the order of the physical world and of the moral world, as well as in the political world. But with regard to the objection based on this fact, to the effect that a great nation [can]not be formed because Lower Canada [is] in great part French and Catholic, and Upper Canada [is] British and Protestant, and the Lower Provinces [are] mixed, it [is] futile and worthless in the extreme. ... In our own Federation, we [will] have Catholic and Protestant, English, French, Irish and Scotch, and each by his efforts and his success [will] increase the prosperity and glory of the new Confederation. [W]e [are] of different races, not for the purpose of warring against each other, but in order to compete and emulate for the general welfare.

The federal-provincial division of powers was a legal recognition of the diversity that existed among the initial members of Confederation, and manifested a concern to accommodate that diversity within a single nation by granting significant powers to provincial governments. The *Constitution Act, 1867* was an act of nation-building. It was the first step in the transition from colonies separately dependent on the Imperial Parliament for their governance to a unified and independent political state in which different peoples could resolve their disagreements and work together toward common goals and a common interest. Federalism was the political mechanism by which diversity could be reconciled with unity.

[44] A federal-provincial division of powers necessitated a written constitution which circumscribed the powers of the new Dominion and Provinces of Canada. Despite its federal structure, the new Dominion was to have "a Constitution similar in Principle to that of the United Kingdom" (*Constitution Act, 1867*, preamble). Allowing for the obvious differences between the governance of Canada and the United Kingdom, it was nevertheless thought important to thus emphasize the continuity of constitutional principles, including democratic institutions and the rule of law; and the continuity of the exercise of sovereign power transferred from Westminster to the federal and provincial capitals of Canada.

[45] After 1867, the Canadian federation continued to evolve both territorially and politically. New territories were admitted to the union and new provinces were formed. In 1870, Rupert's Land and the Northwest Territories were admitted and Manitoba was formed as a province. British Columbia was admitted in 1871, Prince Edward Island in 1873, and the Arctic Islands were added in 1880. In 1898, the Yukon Territory and in 1905, the provinces of Alberta and Saskatchewan were formed from the Northwest Territories. Newfoundland was admitted in 1949 by an amendment to the *Constitution Act, 1867*. The new territory of Nunavut was carved out of the Northwest Territories in 1993 with the partition to become effective in April 1999.

[46] Canada's evolution from colony to fully independent state was gradual. The Imperial Parliament's passage of the *Statute of Westminster, 1931* (U.K.), 22 & 23 Geo. 5, c. 4, confirmed in law what had earlier been confirmed in fact by the Balfour Declaration of 1926, namely, that Canada was an independent country. Thereafter, Canadian law alone governed in Canada, except where Canada expressly consented to the continued application of Imperial legislation. Canada's independence from Britain was achieved through legal and political evolution with an adherence to the rule of law and stability. The proclamation of the *Constitution Act, 1982* removed the last vestige of British authority over the Canadian Constitution

and re-affirmed Canada's commitment to the protection of its minority, aboriginal, equality, legal and language rights, and fundamental freedoms as set out in the *Canadian Charter of Rights and Freedoms*.

[47] Legal continuity, which requires an orderly transfer of authority, necessitated that the 1982 amendments be made by the Westminster Parliament, but the legitimacy as distinguished from the formal legality of the amendments derived from political decisions taken in Canada within a legal framework which this Court, in the *Patriation Reference*, had ruled were in accordance with our Constitution. It should be noted, parenthetically, that the 1982 amendments did not alter the basic division of powers in ss. 91 and 92 of the *Constitution Act, 1867*, which is the primary textual expression of the principle of federalism in our Constitution, agreed upon at Confederation. It did, however, have the important effect that, despite the refusal of the government of Quebec to join in its adoption, Quebec has become bound to the terms of a Constitution that is different from that which prevailed previously, particularly as regards provisions governing its amendment, and the *Canadian Charter of Rights and Freedoms*. As to the latter, to the extent that the scope of legislative powers was thereafter to be constrained by the *Charter*, the constraint operated as much against federal legislative powers as against provincial legislative powers. Moreover, it is to be remembered that s. 33, the "notwithstanding clause", gives Parliament and the provincial legislatures authority to legislate on matters within their jurisdiction in derogation of the fundamental freedoms (s. 2), legal rights (ss. 7 to 14) and equality rights (s. 15) provisions of the *Charter*.

[48] We think it apparent from even this brief historical review that the evolution of our constitutional arrangements has been characterized by adherence to the rule of law, respect for democratic institutions, the accommodation of minorities, insistence that governments adhere to constitutional conduct and a desire for continuity and stability. We now turn to a discussion of the general constitutional principles that bear on the present Reference.

(3) Analysis of the Constitutional Principles

(a) Nature of the Principles

[49] What are those underlying principles? Our Constitution is primarily a written one, the product of 131 years of evolution. Behind the written word is an historical lineage stretching back through the ages, which aids in the consideration of the underlying constitutional

principles. These principles inform and sustain the constitutional text: they are the vital unstated assumptions upon which the text is based. The following discussion addresses the four foundational constitutional principles that are most germane for resolution of this Reference: federalism, democracy, constitutionalism and the rule of law, and respect for minority rights. These defining principles function in symbiosis. No single principle can be defined in isolation from the others, nor does any one principle trump or exclude the operation of any other.

[50] Our Constitution has an internal architecture, or what the majority of this Court in *OPSEU v. Ontario (Attorney General)*, [1987] 2 S.C.R. 2, at p. 57, called a "basic constitutional structure". The individual elements of the Constitution are linked to the others, and must be interpreted by reference to the structure of the Constitution as a whole. As we recently emphasized in the *Provincial Judges Reference*, certain underlying principles infuse our Constitution and breathe life into it. Speaking of the rule of law principle in the *Manitoba Language Rights Reference, supra*, at p. 750, we held that "the principle is clearly implicit in the very nature of a Constitution". The same may be said of the other three constitutional principles we underscore today.

[51] Although these underlying principles are not explicitly made part of the Constitution by any written provision, other than in some respects by the oblique reference in the preamble to the *Constitution Act, 1867*, it would be impossible to conceive of our constitutional structure without them. The principles dictate major elements of the architecture of the Constitution itself and are as such its lifeblood.

[52] The principles assist in the interpretation of the text and the delineation of spheres of jurisdiction, the scope of rights and obligations, and the role of our political institutions. Equally important, observance of and respect for these principles is essential to the ongoing process of constitutional development and evolution of our Constitution as a "living tree", to invoke the famous description in *Edwards v. Attorney-General for Canada*, [1930] A.C. 123 (P.C.), at p. 136. As this Court indicated in *New Brunswick Broadcasting Co. v. Nova Scotia (Speaker of the House of Assembly)*, [1993] 1 S.C.R. 319, Canadians have long recognized the existence and importance of unwritten constitutional principles in our system of government.

[53] Given the existence of these underlying constitutional principles, what use may the Court make of them? In the *Provincial*

Judges Reference, supra, at paras. 93 and 104, we cautioned that the recognition of these constitutional principles (the majority opinion referred to them as "organizing principles" and described one of them, judicial independence, as an "unwritten norm") could not be taken as an invitation to dispense with the written text of the Constitution. On the contrary, we confirmed that there are compelling reasons to insist upon the primacy of our written constitution. A written constitution promotes legal certainty and predictability, and it provides a foundation and a touchstone for the exercise of constitutional judicial review. However, we also observed in the *Provincial Judges Reference* that the effect of the preamble to the *Constitution Act, 1867* was to incorporate certain constitutional principles by reference, a point made earlier in *Fraser v. Public Service Staff Relations Board*, [1985] 2 S.C.R. 455, at pp. 462-63. In the *Provincial Judges Reference*, at para. 104, we determined that the preamble "invites the courts to turn those principles into the premises of a constitutional argument that culminates in the filling of gaps in the express terms of the constitutional text".

[54] Underlying constitutional principles may in certain circumstances give rise to substantive legal obligations (have "full legal force", as we described it in the *Patriation Reference, supra*, at p. 845), which constitute substantive limitations upon government action. These principles may give rise to very abstract and general obligations, or they may be more specific and precise in nature. The principles are not merely descriptive, but are also invested with a powerful normative force, and are binding upon both courts and governments. "In other words", as this Court confirmed in the *Manitoba Language Rights Reference, supra*, at p. 752, "in the process of Constitutional adjudication, the Court may have regard to unwritten postulates which form the very foundation of the Constitution of Canada". It is to a discussion of those underlying constitutional principles that we now turn.

(b) Federalism
[55] It is undisputed that Canada is a federal state. Yet many commentators have observed that, according to the precise terms of the *Constitution Act, 1867*, the federal system was only partial. See, e.g., K. C. Wheare, *Federal Government* (4th ed. 1963), at pp. 18-20. This was so because, on paper, the federal government retained sweeping powers which threatened to undermine the autonomy of the provinces. Here again, however, a review of the written provisions of the

Constitution does not provide the entire picture. Our political and constitutional practice has adhered to an underlying principle of federalism, and has interpreted the written provisions of the Constitution in this light. For example, although the federal power of disallowance was included in the *Constitution Act, 1867*, the underlying principle of federalism triumphed early. Many constitutional scholars contend that the federal power of disallowance has been abandoned (e.g., P. W. Hogg, *Constitutional Law of Canada* (4th ed. 1997), at p. 120).

[56] In a federal system of government such as ours, political power is shared by two orders of government: the federal government on the one hand, and the provinces on the other. Each is assigned respective spheres of jurisdiction by the *Constitution Act, 1867*. See, e.g., *Liquidators of the Maritime Bank of Canada v. Receiver-General of New Brunswick*, [1892] A.C. 437 (P.C.), at pp. 441-42. It is up to the courts "to control the limits of the respective sovereignties": *Northern Telecom Canada Ltd. v. Communication Workers of Canada*, [1983] 1 S.C.R. 733, at p. 741. In interpreting our Constitution, the courts have always been concerned with the federalism principle, inherent in the structure of our constitutional arrangements, which has from the beginning been the lodestar by which the courts have been guided.

[57] This underlying principle of federalism, then, has exercised a role of considerable importance in the interpretation of the written provisions of our Constitution. In the *Patriation Reference, supra*, at pp. 905-9, we confirmed that the principle of federalism runs through the political and legal systems of Canada. Indeed, Martland and Ritchie JJ., dissenting in the *Patriation Reference*, at p. 821, considered federalism to be "the dominant principle of Canadian constitutional law". With the enactment of the *Charter*, that proposition may have less force than it once did, but there can be little doubt that the principle of federalism remains a central organizational theme of our Constitution. Less obviously, perhaps, but certainly of equal importance, federalism is a political and legal response to underlying social and political realities.

[58] The principle of federalism recognizes the diversity of the component parts of Confederation, and the autonomy of provincial governments to develop their societies within their respective spheres of jurisdiction. The federal structure of our country also facilitates democratic participation by distributing power to the government thought to be most suited to achieving the particular societal objec-

tive having regard to this diversity. The scheme of the *Constitution Act, 1867*, it was said in *Re the Initiative and Referendum Act*, [1919] A.C. 935 (P.C.), at p. 942, was

> not to weld the Provinces into one, nor to subordinate Provincial Governments to a central authority, but to establish a central government in which these Provinces should be represented, entrusted with exclusive authority only in affairs in which they had a common interest. Subject to this each Province was to retain its independence and autonomy and to be directly under the Crown as its head.

More recently, in *Haig v. Canada*, [1993] 2 S.C.R. 995, at p. 1047, the majority of this Court held that differences between provinces "are a rational part of the political reality in the federal process". It was referring to the differential application of federal law in individual provinces, but the point applies more generally. A unanimous Court expressed similar views in *R. v. S. (S.)*, [1990] 2 S.C.R. 254, at pp. 287-88.

[59] The principle of federalism facilitates the pursuit of collective goals by cultural and linguistic minorities which form the majority within a particular province. This is the case in Quebec, where the majority of the population is French-speaking, and which possesses a distinct culture. This is not merely the result of chance. The social and demographic reality of Quebec explains the existence of the province of Quebec as a political unit and indeed, was one of the essential reasons for establishing a federal structure for the Canadian union in 1867. The experience of both Canada East and Canada West under the *Union Act, 1840* (U.K.), 3-4 Vict., c. 35, had not been satisfactory. The federal structure adopted at Confederation enabled French-speaking Canadians to form a numerical majority in the province of Quebec, and so exercise the considerable provincial powers conferred by the *Constitution Act, 1867* in such a way as to promote their language and culture. It also made provision for certain guaranteed representation within the federal Parliament itself.

[60] Federalism was also welcomed by Nova Scotia and New Brunswick, both of which also affirmed their will to protect their individual cultures and their autonomy over local matters. All new provinces joining the federation sought to achieve similar objectives, which are no less vigorously pursued by the provinces and territories as we approach the new millenium.

(c) Democracy

[61] Democracy is a fundamental value in our constitutional law and political culture. While it has both an institutional and an individual aspect, the democratic principle was also argued before us in the sense of the supremacy of the sovereign will of a people, in this case potentially to be expressed by Quebecers in support of unilateral secession. It is useful to explore in a summary way these different aspects of the democratic principle.

[62] The principle of democracy has always informed the design of our constitutional structure, and continues to act as an essential interpretive consideration to this day. A majority of this Court in *OPSEU* v. *Ontario, supra*, at p. 57, confirmed that "the basic structure of our Constitution, as established by the Constitution Act, 1867, contemplates the existence of certain political institutions, including freely elected legislative bodies at the federal and provincial levels". As is apparent from an earlier line of decisions emanating from this Court, including *Switzman v. Elbling*, [1957] S.C.R. 285, *Saumur v. City of Quebec*, [1953] 2 S.C.R. 299, *Boucher v. The King*, [1951] S.C.R. 265, and *Reference re Alberta Statutes*, [1938] S.C.R. 100, the democracy principle can best be understood as a sort of baseline against which the framers of our Constitution, and subsequently, our elected representatives under it, have always operated. It is perhaps for this reason that the principle was not explicitly identified in the text of the *Constitution Act, 1867* itself. To have done so might have appeared redundant, even silly, to the framers. As explained in the *Provincial Judges Reference, supra*, at para. 100, it is evident that our Constitution contemplates that Canada shall be a constitutional democracy. Yet this merely demonstrates the importance of underlying constitutional principles that are nowhere explicitly described in our constitutional texts. The representative and democratic nature of our political institutions was simply assumed.

[63] Democracy is commonly understood as being a political system of majority rule. It is essential to be clear what this means. The evolution of our democratic tradition can be traced back to the *Magna Carta* (1215) and before, through the long struggle for Parliamentary supremacy which culminated in the English *Bill of Rights* in 1688-89, the emergence of representative political institutions in the colonial era, the development of responsible government in the 19th century, and eventually, the achievement of Confederation itself in 1867. "[T]he Canadian tradition", the majority of this Court held

in *Reference re Provincial Electoral Boundaries (Sask.)*, [1991] 2 S.C.R. 158, at p. 186, is "one of evolutionary democracy moving in uneven steps toward the goal of universal suffrage and more effective representation". Since Confederation, efforts to extend the franchise to those unjustly excluded from participation in our political system such as women, minorities, and aboriginal peoples have continued, with some success, to the present day.

[64] Democracy is not simply concerned with the process of government. On the contrary, as suggested in *Switzman v. Elbling, supra*, at p. 306, democracy is fundamentally connected to substantive goals, most importantly, the promotion of self-government. Democracy accommodates cultural and group identities: *Reference re Provincial Electoral Boundaries*, at p. 188. Put another way, a sovereign people exercises its right to self-government through the democratic process. In considering the scope and purpose of the *Charter*, the Court in *R. v. Oakes*, [1986] 1 S.C.R. 103, articulated some of the values inherent in the notion of democracy (at p. 136):

> The Court must be guided by the values and principles essential to a free and democratic society which I believe to embody, to name but a few, respect for the inherent dignity of the human person, commitment to social justice and equality, accommodation of a wide variety of beliefs, respect for cultural and group identity, and faith in social and political institutions which enhance the participation of individuals and groups in society.

[65] In institutional terms, democracy means that each of the provincial legislatures and the federal Parliament is elected by popular franchise. These legislatures, we have said, are "at the core of the system of representative government": *New Brunswick Broadcasting, supra*, at p. 387. In individual terms, the right to vote in elections to the House of Commons and the provincial legislatures, and to be candidates in those elections, is guaranteed to "Every citizen of Canada" by virtue of s. 3 of the *Charter*. Historically, this Court has interpreted democracy to mean the process of representative and responsible government and the right of citizens to participate in the political process as voters (*Reference re Provincial Electoral Boundaries, supra*) and as candidates (*Harvey v. New Brunswick (Attorney General)*, [1996] 2 S.C.R. 876). In addition, the effect of s. 4 of the *Charter* is to oblige the House of Commons and the

provincial legislatures to hold regular elections and to permit citizens to elect representatives to their political institutions. The democratic principle is affirmed with particular clarity in that section 4 is not subject to the notwithstanding power contained in s. 33.

[66] It is, of course, true that democracy expresses the sovereign will of the people. Yet this expression, too, must be taken in the context of the other institutional values we have identified as pertinent to this Reference. The relationship between democracy and federalism means, for example, that in Canada there may be different and equally legitimate majorities in different provinces and territories and at the federal level. No one majority is more or less "legitimate" than the others as an expression of democratic opinion, although, of course, the consequences will vary with the subject matter. A federal system of government enables different provinces to pursue policies responsive to the particular concerns and interests of people in that province. At the same time, Canada as a whole is also a democratic community in which citizens construct and achieve goals on a national scale through a federal government acting within the limits of its jurisdiction. The function of federalism is to enable citizens to participate concurrently in different collectivities and to pursue goals at both a provincial and a federal level.

[67] The consent of the governed is a value that is basic to our understanding of a free and democratic society. Yet democracy in any real sense of the word cannot exist without the rule of law. It is the law that creates the framework within which the "sovereign will" is to be ascertained and implemented. To be accorded legitimacy, democratic institutions must rest, ultimately, on a legal foundation. That is, they must allow for the participation of, and accountability to, the people, through public institutions created under the Constitution. Equally, however, a system of government cannot survive through adherence to the law alone. A political system must also possess legitimacy, and in our political culture, that requires an interaction between the rule of law and the democratic principle. The system must be capable of reflecting the aspirations of the people. But there is more. Our law's claim to legitimacy also rests on an appeal to moral values, many of which are imbedded in our constitutional structure. It would be a grave mistake to equate legitimacy with the "sovereign will" or majority rule alone, to the exclusion of other constitutional values.

[68] Finally, we highlight that a functioning democracy requires a continuous process of discussion. The Constitution mandates gov-

ernment by democratic legislatures, and an executive accountable to them, "resting ultimately on public opinion reached by discussion and the interplay of ideas" (*Saumur v. City of Quebec, supra*, at p. 330). At both the federal and provincial level, by its very nature, the need to build majorities necessitates compromise, negotiation, and deliberation. No one has a monopoly on truth, and our system is predicated on the faith that in the marketplace of ideas, the best solutions to public problems will rise to the top. Inevitably, there will be dissenting voices. A democratic system of government is committed to considering those dissenting voices, and seeking to acknowledge and address those voices in the laws by which all in the community must live.

[69] The *Constitution Act, 1982* gives expression to this principle, by conferring a right to initiate constitutional change on each participant in Confederation. In our view, the existence of this right imposes a corresponding duty on the participants in Confederation to engage in constitutional discussions in order to acknowledge and address democratic expressions of a desire for change in other provinces. This duty is inherent in the democratic principle which is a fundamental predicate of our system of governance.

(d) Constitutionalism and the Rule of Law
[70] The principles of constitutionalism and the rule of law lie at the root of our system of government. The rule of law, as observed in *Roncarelli v. Duplessis*, [1959] S.C.R. 121, at p. 142, is "a fundamental postulate of our constitutional structure." As we noted in the *Patriation Reference, supra*, at pp. 805-6, "[t]he 'rule of law' is a highly textured expression, importing many things which are beyond the need of these reasons to explore but conveying, for example, a sense of orderliness, of subjection to known legal rules and of executive accountability to legal authority". At its most basic level, the rule of law vouchsafes to the citizens and residents of the country a stable, predictable and ordered society in which to conduct their affairs. It provides a shield for individuals from arbitrary state action.

[71] In the *Manitoba Language Rights Reference, supra*, at pp. 747-52, this Court outlined the elements of the rule of law. We emphasized, first, that the rule of law provides that the law is supreme over the acts of both government and private persons. There is, in short, one law for all. Second, we explained, at p. 749, that "the rule of law requires the creation and maintenance of an actual order of positive laws which preserves and embodies the more general

principle of normative order". It was this second aspect of the rule
of law that was primarily at issue in the *Manitoba Language Rights
Reference* itself. A third aspect of the rule of law is, as recently
confirmed in the *Provincial Judges Reference, supra*, at para. 10, that
"the exercise of all public power must find its ultimate source in a
legal rule". Put another way, the relationship between the state and
the individual must be regulated by law. Taken together, these three
considerations make up a principle of profound constitutional and
political significance.

[72] The constitutionalism principle bears considerable similarity
to the rule of law, although they are not identical. The essence of
constitutionalism in Canada is embodied in s. 52(1) of the *Constitution Act, 1982*, which provides that "[t]he Constitution of Canada is
the supreme law of Canada, and any law that is inconsistent with the
provisions of the Constitution is, to the extent of the inconsistency,
of no force or effect." Simply put, the constitutionalism principle
requires that all government action comply with the Constitution.
The rule of law principle requires that all government action must
comply with the law, including the Constitution. This Court has
noted on several occasions that with the adoption of the *Charter*, the
Canadian system of government was transformed to a significant
extent from a system of Parliamentary supremacy to one of constitutional supremacy. The Constitution binds all governments, both
federal and provincial, including the executive branch (*Operation
Dismantle Inc. v. The Queen*, [1985] 1 S.C.R. 441, at p. 455). They
may not transgress its provisions: indeed, their sole claim to exercise
lawful authority rests in the powers allocated to them under the
Constitution, and can come from no other source.

[73] An understanding of the scope and importance of the principles of the rule of law and constitutionalism is aided by acknowledging explicitly why a constitution is entrenched beyond the reach
of simple majority rule. There are three overlapping reasons.

[74] First, a constitution may provide an added safeguard for
fundamental human rights and individual freedoms which might
otherwise be susceptible to government interference. Although
democratic government is generally solicitous of those rights, there
are occasions when the majority will be tempted to ignore fundamental rights in order to accomplish collective goals more easily or
effectively. Constitutional entrenchment ensures that those rights
will be given due regard and protection. Second, a constitution may
seek to ensure that vulnerable minority groups are endowed with the

institutions and rights necessary to maintain and promote their identities against the assimilative pressures of the majority. And third, a constitution may provide for a division of political power that allocates political power amongst different levels of government. That purpose would be defeated if one of those democratically elected levels of government could usurp the powers of the other simply by exercising its legislative power to allocate additional political power to itself unilaterally.

[75] The argument that the Constitution may be legitimately circumvented by resort to a majority vote in a province-wide referendum is superficially persuasive, in large measure because it seems to appeal to some of the same principles that underlie the legitimacy of the Constitution itself, namely, democracy and self-government. In short, it is suggested that as the notion of popular sovereignty underlies the legitimacy of our existing constitutional arrangements, so the same popular sovereignty that originally led to the present Constitution must (it is argued) also permit "the people" in their exercise of popular sovereignty to secede by majority vote alone. However, closer analysis reveals that this argument is unsound, because it misunderstands the meaning of popular sovereignty and the essence of a constitutional democracy.

[76] Canadians have never accepted that ours is a system of simple majority rule. Our principle of democracy, taken in conjunction with the other constitutional principles discussed here, is richer. Constitutional government is necessarily predicated on the idea that the political representatives of the people of a province have the capacity and the power to commit the province to be bound into the future by the constitutional rules being adopted. These rules are "binding" not in the sense of frustrating the will of a majority of a province, but as defining the majority which must be consulted in order to alter the fundamental balances of political power (including the spheres of autonomy guaranteed by the principle of federalism), individual rights, and minority rights in our society. Of course, those constitutional rules are themselves amenable to amendment, but only through a process of negotiation which ensures that there is an opportunity for the constitutionally defined rights of all the parties to be respected and reconciled.

[77] In this way, our belief in democracy may be harmonized with our belief in constitutionalism. Constitutional amendment often requires some form of substantial consensus precisely because the content of the underlying principles of our Constitution demand it.

By requiring broad support in the form of an "enhanced majority" to achieve constitutional change, the Constitution ensures that minority interests must be addressed before proposed changes which would affect them may be enacted.

[78] It might be objected, then, that constitutionalism is therefore incompatible with democratic government. This would be an erroneous view. Constitutionalism facilitates — indeed, makes possible — a democratic political system by creating an orderly framework within which people may make political decisions. Viewed correctly, constitutionalism and the rule of law are not in conflict with democracy; rather, they are essential to it. Without that relationship, the political will upon which democratic decisions are taken would itself be undermined.

(e) Protection of Minorities

[79] The fourth underlying constitutional principle we address here concerns the protection of minorities. There are a number of specific constitutional provisions protecting minority language, religion and education rights. Some of those provisions are, as we have recognized on a number of occasions, the product of historical compromises. As this Court observed in *Reference re Bill 30, An Act to amend the Education Act (Ont.)*, [1987] 1 S.C.R. 1148, at p. 1173, and in *Reference re Education Act (Que.)*, [1993] 2 S.C.R. 511, at pp. 529-30, the protection of minority religious education rights was a central consideration in the negotiations leading to Confederation. In the absence of such protection, it was felt that the minorities in what was then Canada East and Canada West would be submerged and assimilated. See also *Greater Montreal Protestant School Board v. Quebec (Attorney General)*, [1989] 1 S.C.R. 377, at pp. 401-2, and *Adler v. Ontario*, [1996] 3 S.C.R. 609. Similar concerns animated the provisions protecting minority language rights, as noted in *Société des Acadiens du Nouveau-Brunswick Inc. v. Association of Parents for Fairness in Education*, [1986] 1 S.C.R. 549, at p. 564.

[80] However, we highlight that even though those provisions were the product of negotiation and political compromise, that does not render them unprincipled. Rather, such a concern reflects a broader principle related to the protection of minority rights. Undoubtedly, the three other constitutional principles inform the scope and operation of the specific provisions that protect the rights of minorities. We emphasize that the protection of minority rights is itself an independent principle underlying our constitutional order.

The principle is clearly reflected in the *Charter's* provisions for the protection of minority rights. See, e.g., *Reference re Public Schools Act (Man.), s. 79(3), (4) and (7)*, [1993] 1 S.C.R. 839, and *Mahe v. Alberta*, [1990] 1 S.C.R. 342.

[81] The concern of our courts and governments to protect minorities has been prominent in recent years, particularly following the enactment of the *Charter*. Undoubtedly, one of the key considerations motivating the enactment of the *Charter*, and the process of constitutional judicial review that it entails, is the protection of minorities. However, it should not be forgotten that the protection of minority rights had a long history before the enactment of the Charter. Indeed, the protection of minority rights was clearly an essential consideration in the design of our constitutional structure even at the time of Confederation: *Senate Reference, supra*, at p. 71. Although Canada's record of upholding the rights of minorities is not a spotless one, that goal is one towards which Canadians have been striving since Confederation, and the process has not been without successes. The principle of protecting minority rights continues to exercise influence in the operation and interpretation of our Constitution.

[82] Consistent with this long tradition of respect for minorities, which is at least as old as Canada itself, the framers of the *Constitution Act, 1982* included in s. 35 explicit protection for existing aboriginal and treaty rights, and in s. 25, a non-derogation clause in favour of the rights of aboriginal peoples. The "promise" of s. 35, as it was termed in *R. v. Sparrow*, [1990] 1 S.C.R. 1075, at p. 1083, recognized not only the ancient occupation of land by aboriginal peoples, but their contribution to the building of Canada, and the special commitments made to them by successive governments. The protection of these rights, so recently and arduously achieved, whether looked at in their own right or as part of the larger concern with minorities, reflects an important underlying constitutional value.

(4) The Operation of the Constitutional Principles in the Secession Context

[83] Secession is the effort of a group or section of a state to withdraw itself from the political and constitutional authority of that state, with a view to achieving statehood for a new territorial unit on the international plane. In a federal state, secession typically takes the form of a territorial unit seeking to withdraw from the federation. Secession is a legal act as much as a political one. By the terms of

Question 1 of this Reference, we are asked to rule on the legality of unilateral secession "under the Constitution of Canada". This is an appropriate question, as the legality of unilateral secession must be evaluated, at least in the first instance, from the perspective of the domestic legal order of the state from which the unit seeks to withdraw. As we shall see below, it is also argued that international law is a relevant standard by which the legality of a purported act of secession may be measured.

[84] The secession of a province from Canada must be considered, in legal terms, to require an amendment to the Constitution, which perforce requires negotiation. The amendments necessary to achieve a secession could be radical and extensive. Some commentators have suggested that secession could be a change of such a magnitude that it could not be considered to be merely an amendment to the Constitution. We are not persuaded by this contention. It is of course true that the Constitution is silent as to the ability of a province to secede from Confederation but, although the Constitution neither expressly authorizes nor prohibits secession, an act of secession would purport to alter the governance of Canadian territory in a manner which undoubtedly is inconsistent with our current constitutional arrangements. The fact that those changes would be profound, or that they would purport to have a significance with respect to international law, does not negate their nature as amendments to the Constitution of Canada.

[85] The Constitution is the expression of the sovereignty of the people of Canada. It lies within the power of the people of Canada, acting through their various governments duly elected and recognized under the Constitution, to effect whatever constitutional arrangements are desired within Canadian territory, including, should it be so desired, the secession of Quebec from Canada. As this Court held in the *Manitoba Language Rights Reference, supra*, at p. 745, "The Constitution of a country is a statement of the will of the people to be governed in accordance with certain principles held as fundamental and certain prescriptions restrictive of the powers of the legislature and government". The manner in which such a political will could be formed and mobilized is a somewhat speculative exercise, though we are asked to assume the existence of such a political will for the purpose of answering the question before us. By the terms of this Reference, we have been asked to consider whether it would be constitutional in such a circumstance for the National Assembly,

legislature or government of Quebec to effect the secession of Quebec from Canada *unilaterally.*

[86] The "unilateral" nature of the act is of cardinal importance and we must be clear as to what is understood by this term. In one sense, any step towards a constitutional amendment initiated by a single actor on the constitutional stage is "unilateral". We do not believe that this is the meaning contemplated by Question 1, nor is this the sense in which the term has been used in argument before us. Rather, what is claimed by a right to secede "unilaterally" is the right to effectuate secession without prior negotiations with the other provinces and the federal government. At issue is not the legality of the first step but the legality of the final act of purported unilateral secession. The supposed juridical basis for such an act is said to be a clear expression of democratic will in a referendum in the province of Quebec. This claim requires us to examine the possible juridical impact, if any, of such a referendum on the functioning of our Constitution, and on the claimed legality of a unilateral act of secession.

[87] Although the Constitution does not itself address the use of a referendum procedure, and the results of a referendum have no direct role or legal effect in our constitutional scheme, a referendum undoubtedly may provide a democratic method of ascertaining the views of the electorate on important political questions on a particular occasion. The democratic principle identified above would demand that considerable weight be given to a clear expression by the people of Quebec of their will to secede from Canada, even though a referendum, in itself and without more, has no direct legal effect, and could not in itself bring about unilateral secession. Our political institutions are premised on the democratic principle, and so an expression of the democratic will of the people of a province carries weight, in that it would confer legitimacy on the efforts of the government of Quebec to initiate the Constitution's amendment process in order to secede by constitutional means. In this context, we refer to a "clear" majority as a qualitative evaluation. The referendum result, if it is to be taken as an expression of the democratic will, must be free of ambiguity both in terms of the question asked and in terms of the support it achieves.

[88] The federalism principle, in conjunction with the democratic principle, dictates that the clear repudiation of the existing constitutional order and the clear expression of the desire to pursue secession by the population of a province would give rise to a reciprocal

obligation on all parties to Confederation to negotiate constitutional changes to respond to that desire. The amendment of the Constitution begins with a political process undertaken pursuant to the Constitution itself. In Canada, the initiative for constitutional amendment is the responsibility of democratically elected representatives of the participants in Confederation. Those representatives may, of course, take their cue from a referendum, but in legal terms, constitution-making in Canada, as in many countries, is undertaken by the democratically elected representatives of the people. The corollary of a legitimate attempt by one participant in Confederation to seek an amendment to the Constitution is an obligation on all parties to come to the negotiating table. The clear repudiation by the people of Quebec of the existing constitutional order would confer legitimacy on demands for secession, and place an obligation on the other provinces and the federal government to acknowledge and respect that expression of democratic will by entering into negotiations and conducting them in accordance with the underlying constitutional principles already discussed.

[89] What is the content of this obligation to negotiate? At this juncture, we confront the difficult inter-relationship between substantive obligations flowing from the Constitution and questions of judicial competence and restraint in supervising or enforcing those obligations. This is mirrored by the distinction between the legality and the legitimacy of actions taken under the Constitution. We propose to focus first on the substantive obligations flowing from this obligation to negotiate; once the nature of those obligations has been described, it is easier to assess the appropriate means of enforcement of those obligations, and to comment on the distinction between legality and legitimacy.

[90] The conduct of the parties in such negotiations would be governed by the same constitutional principles which give rise to the duty to negotiate: federalism, democracy, constitutionalism and the rule of law, and the protection of minorities. Those principles lead us to reject two absolutist propositions. One of those propositions is that there would be a legal obligation on the other provinces and federal government to accede to the secession of a province, subject only to negotiation of the logistical details of secession. This proposition is attributed either to the supposed implications of the democratic principle of the Constitution, or to the international law principle of self-determination of peoples.

[91] For both theoretical and practical reasons, we cannot accept this view. We hold that Quebec could not purport to invoke a right of self-determination such as to dictate the terms of a proposed secession to the other parties: that would not be a negotiation at all. As well, it would be naive to expect that the substantive goal of secession could readily be distinguished from the practical details of secession. The devil would be in the details. The democracy principle, as we have emphasized, cannot be invoked to trump the principles of federalism and rule of law, the rights of individuals and minorities, or the operation of democracy in the other provinces or in Canada as a whole. No negotiations could be effective if their ultimate outcome, secession, is cast as an absolute legal entitlement based upon an obligation to give effect to that act of secession in the Constitution. Such a foregone conclusion would actually undermine the obligation to negotiate and render it hollow.

[92] However, we are equally unable to accept the reverse proposition, that a clear expression of self-determination by the people of Quebec would impose *no* obligations upon the other provinces or the federal government. The continued existence and operation of the Canadian constitutional order cannot remain indifferent to the clear expression of a clear majority of Quebecers that they no longer wish to remain in Canada. This would amount to the assertion that other constitutionally recognized principles necessarily trump the clearly expressed democratic will of the people of Quebec. Such a proposition fails to give sufficient weight to the underlying constitutional principles that must inform the amendment process, including the principles of democracy and federalism. The rights of other provinces and the federal government cannot deny the right of the government of Quebec to pursue secession, should a clear majority of the people of Quebec choose that goal, so long as in doing so, Quebec respects the rights of others. Negotiations would be necessary to address the interests of the federal government, of Quebec and the other provinces, and other participants, as well as the rights of *all* Canadians both within and outside Quebec.

[93] Is the rejection of both of these propositions reconcilable? Yes, once it is realized that none of the rights or principles under discussion is absolute to the exclusion of the others. This observation suggests that other parties cannot exercise their rights in such a way as to amount to an absolute denial of Quebec's rights, and similarly, that so long as Quebec exercises its rights while respecting the rights of others, it may propose secession and seek to achieve it through

negotiation. The negotiation process precipitated by a decision of a clear majority of the population of Quebec on a clear question to pursue secession would require the reconciliation of various rights and obligations by the representatives of two legitimate majorities, namely, the clear majority of the population of Quebec, and the clear majority of Canada as a whole, whatever that may be. There can be no suggestion that either of these majorities "trumps" the other. A political majority that does not act in accordance with the underlying constitutional principles we have identified puts at risk the legitimacy of the exercise of its rights.

[94] In such circumstances, the conduct of the parties assumes primary constitutional significance. The negotiation process must be conducted with an eye to the constitutional principles we have outlined, which must inform the actions of *all* the participants in the negotiation process.

[95] Refusal of a party to conduct negotiations in a manner consistent with constitutional principles and values would seriously put at risk the legitimacy of that party's assertion of its rights, and perhaps the negotiation process as a whole. Those who quite legitimately insist upon the importance of upholding the rule of law cannot at the same time be oblivious to the need to act in conformity with constitutional principles and values, and so do their part to contribute to the maintenance and promotion of an environment in which the rule of law may flourish.

[96] No one can predict the course that such negotiations might take. The possibility that they might not lead to an agreement amongst the parties must be recognized. Negotiations following a referendum vote in favour of seeking secession would inevitably address a wide range of issues, many of great import. After 131 years of Confederation, there exists, inevitably, a high level of integration in economic, political and social institutions across Canada. The vision of those who brought about Confederation was to create a unified country, not a loose alliance of autonomous provinces. Accordingly, while there are regional economic interests, which sometimes coincide with provincial boundaries, there are also national interests and enterprises (both public and private) that would face potential dismemberment. There is a national economy and a national debt. Arguments were raised before us regarding boundary issues. There are linguistic and cultural minorities, including aboriginal peoples, unevenly distributed across the country who look to the Constitution of Canada for the protection of their rights. Of course,

secession would give rise to many issues of great complexity and difficulty. These would have to be resolved within the overall framework of the rule of law, thereby assuring Canadians resident in Quebec and elsewhere a measure of stability in what would likely be a period of considerable upheaval and uncertainty. Nobody seriously suggests that our national existence, seamless in so many aspects, could be effortlessly separated along what are now the provincial boundaries of Quebec. As the Attorney General of Saskatchewan put it in his oral submission:

> A nation is built when the communities that comprise it make commitments to it, when they forego choices and opportunities on behalf of a nation, ... when the communities that comprise it make compromises, when they offer each other guarantees, when they make transfers and perhaps most pointedly, when they receive from others the benefits of national solidarity. The threads of a thousand acts of accommodation are the fabric of a nation.

[97] In the circumstances, negotiations following such a referendum would undoubtedly be difficult. While the negotiators would have to contemplate the possibility of secession, there would be no absolute legal entitlement to it and no assumption that an agreement reconciling all relevant rights and obligations would actually be reached. It is foreseeable that even negotiations carried out in conformity with the underlying constitutional principles could reach an impasse. We need not speculate here as to what would then transpire. Under the Constitution, secession requires that an amendment be negotiated.

[98] The respective roles of the courts and political actors in discharging the constitutional obligations we have identified follows ineluctably from the foregoing observations. In the *Patriation Reference*, a distinction was drawn between the law of the Constitution, which, generally speaking, will be enforced by the courts, and other constitutional rules, such as the conventions of the Constitution, which carry only political sanctions. It is also the case, however, that judicial intervention, even in relation to the *law* of the Constitution, is subject to the Court's appreciation of its proper role in the constitutional scheme.

[99] The notion of justiciability is, as we earlier pointed out in dealing with the preliminary objection, linked to the notion of appro-

priate judicial restraint. We earlier made reference to the discussion of justiciability in *Reference re Canada Assistance Plan, supra*, at p. 545:

> In exercising its discretion whether to determine a matter that is alleged to be non-justiciable, the Court's primary concern is to retain its proper role within the constitutional framework of our democratic form of government.

In *Operation Dismantle, supra*, at p. 459, it was pointed out that justiciability is a "doctrine ... founded upon a concern with the appropriate role of the courts as the forum for the resolution of different types of disputes". An analogous doctrine of judicial restraint operates here. Also, as observed in *Canada (Auditor General) v. Canada (Minister of Energy, Mines and Resources)*, [1989] 2 S.C.R. 49 (the *Auditor General*'s case), at p. 91:

> There is an array of issues which calls for the exercise of judicial judgment on whether the questions are properly cognizable by the courts. Ultimately, such judgment depends on the appreciation by the judiciary of its own position in the constitutional scheme.

[100] The role of the Court in this Reference is limited to the identification of the relevant aspects of the Constitution in their broadest sense. We have interpreted the questions as relating to the constitutional framework within which political decisions may ultimately be made. Within that framework, the workings of the political process are complex and can only be resolved by means of political judgments and evaluations. The Court has no supervisory role over the political aspects of constitutional negotiations. Equally, the initial impetus for negotiation, namely a clear majority on a clear question in favour of secession, is subject only to political evaluation, and properly so. A right and a corresponding duty to negotiate secession cannot be built on an alleged expression of democratic will if the expression of democratic will is itself fraught with ambiguities. Only the political actors would have the information and expertise to make the appropriate judgment as to the point at which, and the circumstances in which, those ambiguities are resolved one way or the other.

[101] If the circumstances giving rise to the duty to negotiate were to arise, the distinction between the strong defence of legitimate

interests and the taking of positions which, in fact, ignore the legitimate interests of others is one that also defies legal analysis. The Court would not have access to all of the information available to the political actors, and the methods appropriate for the search for truth in a court of law are ill-suited to getting to the bottom of constitutional negotiations. To the extent that the questions are political in nature, it is not the role of the judiciary to interpose its own views on the different negotiating positions of the parties, even were it invited to do so. Rather, it is the obligation of the elected representatives to give concrete form to the discharge of their constitutional obligations which only they and their electors can ultimately assess. The reconciliation of the various legitimate constitutional interests outlined above is necessarily committed to the political rather than the judicial realm, precisely because that reconciliation can only be achieved through the give and take of the negotiation process. Having established the legal framework, it would be for the democratically elected leadership of the various participants to resolve their differences.

[102] The non-justiciability of political issues that lack a legal component does not deprive the surrounding constitutional framework of its binding status, nor does this mean that constitutional obligations could be breached without incurring serious legal repercussions. Where there are legal rights there are remedies, but as we explained in the *Auditor General*'s case, *supra*, at p. 90, and *New Brunswick Broadcasting, supra*, the appropriate recourse in some circumstances lies through the workings of the political process rather than the courts.

[103] To the extent that a breach of the constitutional duty to negotiate in accordance with the principles described above undermines the legitimacy of a party's actions, it may have important ramifications at the international level. Thus, a failure of the duty to undertake negotiations and pursue them according to constitutional principles may undermine that government's claim to legitimacy which is generally a precondition for recognition by the international community. Conversely, violations of those principles by the federal or other provincial governments responding to the request for secession may undermine their legitimacy. Thus, a Quebec that had negotiated in conformity with constitutional principles and values in the face of unreasonable intransigence on the part of other participants at the federal or provincial level would be more likely to be recognized than a Quebec which did not itself act according to constitu-

tional principles in the negotiation process. Both the legality of the acts of the parties to the negotiation process under Canadian law, and the perceived legitimacy of such action, would be important considerations in the recognition process. In this way, the adherence of the parties to the obligation to negotiate would be evaluated in an indirect manner on the international plane.

[104] Accordingly, the secession of Quebec from Canada cannot be accomplished by the National Assembly, the legislature or government of Quebec unilaterally, that is to say, without principled negotiations, and be considered a lawful act. Any attempt to effect the secession of a province from Canada must be undertaken pursuant to the Constitution of Canada, or else violate the Canadian legal order. However, the continued existence and operation of the Canadian constitutional order cannot remain unaffected by the unambiguous expression of a clear majority of Quebecers that they no longer wish to remain in Canada. The primary means by which that expression is given effect is the constitutional duty to negotiate in accordance with the constitutional principles that we have described herein. In the event secession negotiations are initiated, our Constitution, no less than our history, would call on the participants to work to reconcile the rights, obligations and legitimate aspirations of all Canadians within a framework that emphasizes constitutional responsibilities as much as it does constitutional rights.

[105] It will be noted that Question 1 does not ask how secession could be achieved in a constitutional manner, but addresses one form of secession only, namely unilateral secession. Although the applicability of various procedures to achieve lawful secession was raised in argument, each option would require us to assume the existence of facts that at this stage are unknown. In accordance with the usual rule of prudence in constitutional cases, we refrain from pronouncing on the applicability of any particular constitutional procedure to effect secession unless and until sufficiently clear facts exist to squarely raise an issue for judicial determination.

(5) Suggested Principle of Effectivity
[106] In the foregoing discussion we have not overlooked the principle of effectivity, which was placed at the forefront in argument before us. For the reasons that follow, we do not think that the principle of effectivity has any application to the issues raised by Question 1. A distinction must be drawn between the right of a people to act, and their power to do so. They are not identical. A

right is recognized in law: mere physical ability is not necessarily given status as a right. The fact that an individual or group can act in a certain way says nothing at all about the legal status or consequences of the act. A power may be exercised even in the absence of a right to do so, but if it is, then it is exercised without legal foundation. Our Constitution does not address powers in this sense. On the contrary, the Constitution is concerned only with the rights and obligations of individuals, groups and governments, and the structure of our institutions. It was suggested before us that the National Assembly, legislature or government of Quebec could unilaterally effect the secession of that province from Canada, but it was not suggested that they might do so as a matter of law: rather, it was contended that they simply could do so as a matter of fact. Although under the Constitution there is no right to pursue secession unilaterally, that is secession without principled negotiation, this does not rule out the possibility of an unconstitutional declaration of secession leading to a *de facto* secession. The ultimate success of such a secession would be dependent on effective control of a territory and recognition by the international community. The principles governing secession at international law are discussed in our answer to Question 2.

[107] In our view, the alleged principle of effectivity has no constitutional or legal status in the sense that it does not provide an *ex ante* explanation or justification for an act. In essence, acceptance of a principle of effectivity would be tantamount to accepting that the National Assembly, legislature or government of Quebec may act without regard to the law, simply because it asserts the power to do so. So viewed, the suggestion is that the National Assembly, legislature or government of Quebec could purport to secede the province unilaterally from Canada in disregard of Canadian and international law. It is further suggested that if the secession bid was successful, a new legal order would be created in that province, which would then be considered an independent state.

[108] Such a proposition is an assertion of fact, not a statement of law. It may or may not be true; in any event it is irrelevant to the questions of law before us. If, on the other hand, it is put forward as an assertion of law, then it simply amounts to the contention that the law may be broken as long as it can be broken successfully. Such a notion is contrary to the rule of law, and must be rejected.

B. Question 2

> Does international law give the National Assembly, legislature or government of Quebec the right to effect the secession of Quebec from Canada unilaterally? In this regard, is there a right to self-determination under international law that would give the National Assembly, legislature or government of Quebec the right to effect the secession of Quebec from Canada unilaterally?

[109] For reasons already discussed, the Court does not accept the contention that Question 2 raises a question of "pure" international law which this Court has no jurisdiction to address. Question 2 is posed in the context of a Reference to address the existence or non-existence of a right of unilateral secession by a province of Canada. The *amicus curiae* argues that this question ultimately falls to be determined under international law. In addressing this issue, the Court does not purport to act as an arbiter between sovereign states or more generally within the international community. The Court is engaged in rendering an advisory opinion on certain legal aspects of the continued existence of the Canadian federation. International law has been invoked as a consideration and it must therefore be addressed.

[110] The argument before the Court on Question 2 has focused largely on determining whether, under international law, a positive legal right to unilateral secession exists in the factual circumstances assumed for the purpose of our response to Question 1. Arguments were also advanced to the effect that, regardless of the existence or non-existence of a positive right to unilateral secession, international law will in the end recognize effective political realities — including the emergence of a new state — as facts. While our response to Question 2 will address considerations raised by this alternative argument of "effectivity", it should first be noted that the existence of a positive legal entitlement is quite different from a prediction that the law will respond after the fact to a then existing political reality. These two concepts examine different points in time. The questions posed to the Court address legal rights in advance of a unilateral act of purported secession. While we touch below on the practice governing the international recognition of emerging states, the Court is as wary of entertaining speculation about the possible future conduct of sovereign states on the international level as it was under Question 1 to speculate about the possible future course of political negotia-

tions among the participants in the Canadian federation. In both cases, the Reference questions are directed only to the *legal* framework within which the political actors discharge their various mandates.

(1) Secession at International Law

[111] It is clear that international law does not specifically grant component parts of sovereign states the legal right to secede unilaterally from their "parent" state. This is acknowledged by the experts who provided their opinions on behalf of both the *amicus curiae* and the Attorney General of Canada. Given the lack of specific authorization for unilateral secession, proponents of the existence of such a right at international law are therefore left to attempt to found their argument (i) on the proposition that unilateral secession is not specifically prohibited and that what is not specifically prohibited is inferentially permitted; or (ii) on the implied duty of states to recognize the legitimacy of secession brought about by the exercise of the well-established international law right of "a people" to self-determination. The *amicus curiae* addressed the right of self-determination, but submitted that it was not applicable to the circumstances of Quebec within the Canadian federation, irrespective of the existence or non-existence of a referendum result in favour of secession. We agree on this point with the *amicus curiae*, for reasons that we will briefly develop.

(a) Absence of a Specific Prohibition

[112] International law contains neither a right of unilateral secession nor the explicit denial of such a right, although such a denial is, to some extent, implicit in the exceptional circumstances required for secession to be permitted under the right of a people to self-determination, e.g., the right of secession that arises in the exceptional situation of an oppressed or colonial people, discussed below. As will be seen, international law places great importance on the territorial integrity of nation states and, by and large, leaves the creation of a new state to be determined by the domestic law of the existing state of which the seceding entity presently forms a part (R. Y. Jennings, *The Acquisition of Territory in International Law* (1963) at pp. 8-9). Where, as here, unilateral secession would be incompatible with the domestic Constitution, international law is likely to accept that conclusion subject to the right of peoples to self-determination, a topic to which we now turn.

(b) The Right of a People to Self-determination
[113] While international law generally regulates the conduct of nation states, it does, in some specific circumstances, also recognize the "rights" of entities other than nation states — such as the right of a *people* to self-determination.

[114] The existence of the right of a people to self-determination is now so widely recognized in international conventions that the principle has acquired a status beyond "convention" and is considered a general principle of international law (A. Cassese, *Self-determination of peoples: A legal reappraisal* (1995), at pp. 171-72; K. Doehring, "Self- Determination", in B. Simma, ed., *The Charter of the United Nations: A Commentary* (1994), at p. 70).

[115] Article 1 of the *Charter of the United Nations*, Can. T.S. 1945 No. 7, states in part that one of the purposes of the United Nations (U.N.) is:

Article 1

...

2. To develop friendly relations among nations based on respect for the principle of equal rights and self-determination of peoples, and to take other appropriate measures to strengthen universal peace;

[116] Article 55 of the U.N. Charter further states that the U.N. shall promote goals such as higher standards of living, full employment and human rights "[w]ith a view to the creation of conditions of stability and well-being which are necessary for peaceful and friendly relations among nations based on respect for the principle of equal rights and self-determination of peoples".

[117] This basic principle of self-determination has been carried forward and addressed in so many U.N. conventions and resolutions that, as noted by Doehring, *supra*, at p. 60:

The sheer number of resolutions concerning the right of self-determination makes their enumeration impossible.

[118] For our purposes, reference to the following conventions and resolutions is sufficient. Article 1 of both the U.N.'s *International Covenant on Civil and Political Rights*, 999 U.N.T.S. 171, and

its *International Covenant on Economic, Social and Cultural Rights*, 993 U.N.T.S. 3, states:

> 1. All peoples have the right of self-determination. By virtue of that right they freely determine their political status and freely pursue their economic, social and cultural development.

[119] Similarly, the U.N. General Assembly's *Declaration on Principles of International Law Concerning Friendly Relations and Co-operation Among States in Accordance with the Charter of the United Nations*, GA Res. 2625 (XXV), 24 October 1970 (*Declaration on Friendly Relations*), states:

> By virtue of the principle of equal rights and self-determination of peoples enshrined in the Charter of the United Nations, all peoples have the right freely to determine, without external interference, their political status and to pursue their economic, social and cultural development, and every State has the duty to respect this right in accordance with the provisions of the Charter.

[120] In 1993, the U.N. World Conference on Human Rights adopted the *Vienna Declaration and Programme of Action*, A/Conf. 157/24, 25 June 1993, that reaffirmed Article 1 of the two above-mentioned covenants. The U.N. General Assembly's *Declaration on the Occasion of the Fiftieth Anniversary of the United Nations*, GA Res. 50/6, 9 November 1995, also emphasizes the right to self-determination by providing that the U.N.'s member states will:

> 1. ...Continue to reaffirm the right of *self-determination of all peoples*, taking into account the particular situation of peoples under colonial or other forms of alien domination or foreign occupation, and recognize the right of peoples to take legitimate action in accordance with the Charter of the United Nations to realize their inalienable right of self-determination. *This shall not be construed as authorizing* or encouraging any action that would dismember or impair, totally or in part, the *territorial integrity or political unity of sovereign and independent States* conducting themselves in compliance with the principle of equal rights and self-determination of peoples and thus possessed of a Government representing the whole people belong-

ing to the territory without distinction of any kind. ... [Emphasis added.]

[121] The right to self-determination is also recognized in other international legal documents. For example, the *Final Act of the Conference on Security and Co-operation in Europe*, 14 I.L.M. 1292 (1975) (*Helsinki Final Act*), states (in Part VIII):

> The participating States will respect the equal rights of peoples and *their right to self-determination*, acting at all times in conformity with the purposes and principles of the Charter of the United Nations and with the relevant norms of international law, including those relating to territorial integrity of States.

> By virtue of the principle of equal rights and self-determination of peoples, all peoples always have the right, in full freedom, to determine, when and as they wish, their internal and external political status, without external interference, and to pursue as they wish their political, economic, social and cultural development. [Emphasis added.]

[122] As will be seen, international law expects that the right to self-determination will be exercised by peoples within the framework of existing sovereign states and consistently with the maintenance of the territorial integrity of those states. Where this is not possible, in the exceptional circumstances discussed below, a right of secession may arise.

(i) Defining "Peoples"

[123] International law grants the right to self-determination to "peoples". Accordingly, access to the right requires the threshold step of characterizing as a people the group seeking self-determination. However, as the right to self-determination has developed by virtue of a combination of international agreements and conventions, coupled with state practice, with little formal elaboration of the definition of "peoples", the result has been that the precise meaning of the term "people" remains somewhat uncertain.

[124] It is clear that "a people" may include only a portion of the population of an existing state. The right to self-determination has developed largely as a human right, and is generally used in documents that simultaneously contain references to "nation" and "state". The juxtaposition of these terms is indicative that the reference to

"people" does not necessarily mean the entirety of a state's population. To restrict the definition of the term to the population of existing states would render the granting of a right to self-determination largely duplicative, given the parallel emphasis within the majority of the source documents on the need to protect the territorial integrity of existing states, and would frustrate its remedial purpose.

[125] While much of the Quebec population certainly shares many of the characteristics (such as a common language and culture) that would be considered in determining whether a specific group is a "people", as do other groups within Quebec and/or Canada, it is not necessary to explore this legal characterization to resolve Question 2 appropriately. Similarly, it is not necessary for the Court to determine whether, should a Quebec people exist within the definition of public international law, such a people encompasses the entirety of the provincial population or just a portion thereof. Nor is it necessary to examine the position of the aboriginal population within Quebec. As the following discussion of the scope of the right to self-determination will make clear, whatever be the correct application of the definition of people(s) in this context, their right of self-determination cannot in the present circumstances be said to ground a right to unilateral secession.

(ii) Scope of the Right to Self-determination

[126] The recognized sources of international law establish that the right to self-determination of a people is normally fulfilled through *internal* self-determination — a people's pursuit of its political, economic, social and cultural development within the framework of an existing state. A right to *external* self-determination (which in this case potentially takes the form of the assertion of a right to unilateral secession) arises in only the most extreme of cases and, even then, under carefully defined circumstances. *External* self-determination can be defined as in the following statement from the *Declaration on Friendly Relations, supra*, as

> The establishment of a sovereign and independent State, the free association or integration with an independent State or the emergence into any other political status freely determined by a *people* constitute modes of implementing the right of self-determination by *that people*. [Emphasis added.]

[127] The international law principle of self-determination has evolved within a framework of respect for the territorial integrity of

existing states. The various international documents that support the existence of a people's right to self-determination also contain parallel statements supportive of the conclusion that the exercise of such a right must be sufficiently limited to prevent threats to an existing state's territorial integrity or the stability of relations between sovereign states.

[128] The *Declaration on Friendly Relations, supra*, the *Vienna Declaration, supra*, and the *Declaration on the Occasion of the Fiftieth Anniversary of the United Nations, supra*, are specific. They state, immediately after affirming a people's right to determine political, economic, social and cultural issues, that such rights are not to

> be construed as authorizing or encouraging any action which would dismember or impair, totally or in part, the territorial integrity or political unity of sovereign and independent States conducting themselves in compliance with the principle of equal rights and self-determination of peoples as described above and thus possessed of a government representing the whole people belonging to the territory without distinction ... [Emphasis added.]

[129] Similarly, while the concluding document of the Vienna Meeting in 1989 of the Conference on Security and Co-operation in Europe on the follow-up to the *Helsinki Final Act* again refers to peoples having the right to determine "their internal and *external* political status" (emphasis added), that statement is immediately followed by express recognition that the participating states will at all times act, as stated in the *Helsinki Final Act*, "in conformity with the purposes and principles of the Charter of the United Nations and with the relevant norms of international law, *including those relating to territorial integrity of states*" (emphasis added). Principle 5 of the concluding document states that the participating states (including Canada):

> ... confirm their commitment strictly and effectively to observe the principle of the territorial integrity of States. They will refrain from any violation of this principle and thus from any action aimed by direct or indirect means, in contravention of the purposes and principles of the Charter of the United Nations, other obligations under international law or the provisions of the [Helsinki] Final Act, at violating the territorial

integrity, political independence or the unity of a State. *No actions or situations in contravention of this principle will be recognized as legal by the participating States.* [Emphasis added.]

Accordingly, the reference in the *Helsinki Final Act* to a people determining its external political status is interpreted to mean the expression of a people's external political status through the government of the existing state, save in the exceptional circumstances discussed below. As noted by Cassese, *supra*, at p. 287, given the history and textual structure of this document, its reference to external self-determination simply means that "no territorial or other change can be brought about by the central authorities of a State that is contrary to the will of the whole people of that State".

[130] While the *International Covenant on Economic, Social and Cultural Rights, supra*, and the *International Covenant on Civil and Political Rights, supra*, do not specifically refer to the protection of territorial integrity, they both define the ambit of the right to self-determination in terms that are normally attainable within the framework of an existing state. There is no necessary incompatibility between the maintenance of the territorial integrity of existing states, including Canada, and the right of a "people" to achieve a full measure of self-determination. A state whose government represents the whole of the people or peoples resident within its territory, on a basis of equality and without discrimination, and respects the principles of self-determination in its own internal arrangements, is entitled to the protection under international law of its territorial integrity.

(iii) Colonial and Oppressed Peoples

[131] Accordingly, the general state of international law with respect to the right to self-determination is that the right operates within the overriding protection granted to the territorial integrity of "parent" states. However, as noted by Cassese, supra, at p. 334, there are certain defined contexts within which the right to the self-determination of peoples does allow that right to be exercised "externally", which, in the context of this Reference, would potentially mean secession:

... the right to external self-determination, which entails the possibility of choosing (or restoring) independence, has only been bestowed upon two classes of peoples (those under colonial rule or foreign occupation), based upon the assumption that both classes make up entities that are inherently distinct from the colonialist Power and the occupant Power and that their 'territorial integrity', all but destroyed by the colonialist or occupying Power, should be fully restored....

[132] The right of colonial peoples to exercise their right to self-determination by breaking away from the "imperial" power is now undisputed, but is irrelevant to this Reference.

[133] The other clear case where a right to external self-determination accrues is where a people is subject to alien subjugation, domination or exploitation outside a colonial context. This recognition finds its roots in the *Declaration on Friendly Relations, supra*:

Every State has the duty to promote, through joint and separate action, the realization of the principle of equal rights and self-determination of peoples, in accordance with the provisions of the Charter, and to render assistance to the United Nations in carrying out the responsibilities entrusted to it by the Charter regarding the implementation of the principle, in order:

(a) To promote friendly relations and co-operation among States; and

(b) To bring a speedy end to colonialism, having due regard to the freely expressed will of the peoples concerned;

and bearing in mind that subjection of peoples to alien subjugation, domination and exploitation constitutes a violation of the principle, as well as a denial of fundamental human rights, and is contrary to the Charter of the United Nations.

[134] A number of commentators have further asserted that the right to self-determination may ground a right to unilateral secession in a third circumstance. Although this third circumstance has been described in several ways, the underlying proposition is that, when a people is blocked from the meaningful exercise of its right to self-determination internally, it is entitled, as a last resort, to exercise it by secession. The *Vienna Declaration, supra*, requirement that governments represent "the whole people belonging to the territory without distinction of any kind" adds credence to the assertion that

such a complete blockage may potentially give rise to a right of secession.

[135] Clearly, such a circumstance parallels the other two recognized situations in that the ability of a people to exercise its right to self-determination internally is somehow being totally frustrated. While it remains unclear whether this third proposition actually reflects an established international law standard, it is unnecessary for present purposes to make that determination. Even assuming that the third circumstance is sufficient to create a right to unilateral secession under international law, the current Quebec context cannot be said to approach such a threshold. As stated by the *amicus curiae*, Addendum to the factum of the *amicus curiae*, at paras. 15-16:

> [translation] 15. The Quebec people is not the victim of attacks on its physical existence or integrity, or of a massive violation of its fundamental rights. The Quebec people is manifestly not, in the opinion of the *amicus curiae*, an oppressed people.

> 16. For close to 40 of the last 50 years, the Prime Minister of Canada has been a Quebecer. During this period, Quebecers have held from time to time all the most important positions in the federal Cabinet. During the 8 years prior to June 1997, the Prime Minister and the Leader of the Official Opposition in the House of Commons were both Quebecers. At present, the Prime Minister of Canada, the Right Honourable Chief Justice and two other members of the Court, the Chief of Staff of the Canadian Armed Forces and the Canadian ambassador to the United States, not to mention the Deputy Secretary-General of the United Nations, are all Quebecers. The international achievements of Quebecers in most fields of human endeavour are too numerous to list. Since the dynamism of the Quebec people has been directed toward the business sector, it has been clearly successful in Quebec, the rest of Canada and abroad.

[136] The population of Quebec cannot plausibly be said to be denied access to government. Quebecers occupy prominent positions within the government of Canada. Residents of the province freely make political choices and pursue economic, social and cultural development within Quebec, across Canada, and throughout the world. The population of Quebec is equitably represented in legislative, executive and judicial institutions. In short, to reflect the phra-

seology of the international documents that address the right to self-determination of peoples, Canada is a "sovereign and independent state conducting itself in compliance with the principle of equal rights and self-determination of peoples and thus possessed of a government representing the whole people belonging to the territory without distinction".

[137] The continuing failure to reach agreement on amendments to the Constitution, while a matter of concern, does not amount to a denial of self-determination. In the absence of amendments to the Canadian Constitution, we must look at the constitutional arrangements presently in effect, and we cannot conclude under current circumstances that those arrangements place Quebecers in a disadvantaged position within the scope of the international law rule.

[138] In summary, the international law right to self-determination only generates, at best, a right to external self-determination in situations of former colonies; where a people is oppressed, as for example under foreign military occupation; or where a definable group is denied meaningful access to government to pursue their political, economic, social and cultural development. In all three situations, the people in question are entitled to a right to external self-determination because they have been denied the ability to exert internally their right to self-determination. Such exceptional circumstances are manifestly inapplicable to Quebec under existing conditions. Accordingly, neither the population of the province of Quebec, even if characterized in terms of "people" or "peoples", nor its representative institutions, the National Assembly, the legislature or government of Quebec, possess a right, under international law, to secede unilaterally from Canada.

[139] We would not wish to leave this aspect of our answer to Question 2 without acknowledging the importance of the submissions made to us respecting the rights and concerns of aboriginal peoples in the event of a unilateral secession, as well as the appropriate means of defining the boundaries of a seceding Quebec with particular regard to the northern lands occupied largely by aboriginal peoples. However, the concern of aboriginal peoples is precipitated by the asserted right of Quebec to unilateral secession. In light of our finding that there is no such right applicable to the population of Quebec, either under the Constitution of Canada or at international law, but that on the contrary a clear democratic expression of support for secession would lead under the Constitution to negotiations in which aboriginal interests would be taken into account, it becomes

unnecessary to explore further the concerns of the aboriginal peoples in this Reference.

(2) Recognition of a Factual/Political Reality: the "Effectivity" Principle

[140] As stated, an argument advanced by the *amicus curiae* on this branch of the Reference was that, while international law may not ground a positive right to unilateral secession in the context of Quebec, international law equally does not prohibit secession and, in fact, international recognition would be conferred on such a political reality if it emerged, for example, via effective control of the territory of what is now the province of Quebec.

[141] It is true that international law may well, depending on the circumstances, adapt to recognize a political and/or factual reality, regardless of the legality of the steps leading to its creation. However, as mentioned at the outset, effectivity, as such, does not have any real applicability to Question 2, which asks whether a *right* to unilateral secession exists.

[142] No one doubts that legal consequences may flow from political facts, and that "sovereignty is a political fact for which no purely legal authority can be constituted ...", H. W. R. Wade, "The Basis of Legal Sovereignty", [1955] *Camb. L.J.* 172, at p. 196. Secession of a province from Canada, if successful in the streets, might well lead to the creation of a new state. Although recognition by other states is not, at least as a matter of theory, necessary to achieve statehood, the viability of a would-be state in the international community depends, as a practical matter, upon recognition by other states. That process of recognition is guided by legal norms. However, international recognition is not alone constitutive of statehood and, critically, does not relate back to the date of secession to serve retroactively as a source of a "legal" right to secede in the first place. Recognition occurs only after a territorial unit has been successful, as a political fact, in achieving secession.

[143] As indicated in responding to Question 1, one of the legal norms which may be recognized by states in granting or withholding recognition of emergent states is the legitimacy of the process by which the *de facto* secession is, or was, being pursued. The process of recognition, once considered to be an exercise of pure sovereign discretion, has come to be associated with legal norms. See, e.g., European Community Declaration on the *Guidelines on the Recognition of New States in Eastern Europe and in the Soviet Union*, 31

I.L.M. 1486 (1992), at p. 1487. While national interest and perceived political advantage to the recognizing state obviously play an important role, foreign states may also take into account their view as to the existence of a right to self-determination on the part of the population of the putative state, and a counterpart domestic evaluation, namely, an examination of the legality of the secession according to the law of the state from which the territorial unit purports to have seceded. As we indicated in our answer to Question 1, an emergent state that has disregarded legitimate obligations arising out of its previous situation can potentially expect to be hindered by that disregard in achieving international recognition, at least with respect to the timing of that recognition. On the other hand, compliance by the seceding province with such legitimate obligations would weigh in favour of international recognition. The notion that what is not explicitly prohibited is implicitly permitted has little relevance where (as here) international law refers the legality of secession to the domestic law of the seceding state and the law of that state holds unilateral secession to be unconstitutional.

[144] As a court of law, we are ultimately concerned only with legal claims. If the principle of "effectivity" is no more than that "successful revolution begets its own legality" (S. A. de Smith, "Constitutional Lawyers in Revolutionary Situations" (1968), 7 *West. Ont. L. Rev.* 93, at p. 96), it necessarily means that legality follows and does not precede the successful revolution. *Ex hypothesi*, the successful revolution took place outside the constitutional framework of the predecessor state, otherwise it would not be characterized as "a revolution". It may be that a unilateral secession by Quebec would eventually be accorded legal status by Canada and other states, and thus give rise to legal consequences; but this does not support the more radical contention that subsequent recognition of a state of affairs brought about by a unilateral declaration of independence could be taken to mean that secession was achieved under colour of a legal right.

[145] An argument was made to analogize the principle of effectivity with the second aspect of the rule of law identified by this Court in the *Manitoba Language Rights Reference, supra*, at p. 753, namely, avoidance of a legal vacuum. In that Reference, it will be recalled, this Court declined to strike down all of Manitoba's legislation for its failure to comply with constitutional dictates, out of concern that this would leave the province in a state of chaos. In so doing, we recognized that the rule of law is a constitutional principle

which permits the courts to address the practical consequences of their actions, particularly in constitutional cases. The similarity between that principle and the principle of effectivity, it was argued, is that both attempt to refashion the law to meet social reality. However, nothing of our concern in the *Manitoba Language Rights Reference* about the severe practical consequences of unconstitutionality affected our conclusion that, as a matter of law, all Manitoba legislation at issue in that case was unconstitutional. The Court's declaration of unconstitutionality was clear and unambiguous. The Court's concern with maintenance of the rule of law was directed in its relevant aspect to the appropriate remedy, which in that case was to suspend the declaration of invalidity to permit appropriate rectification to take place.

[146] The principle of effectivity operates very differently. It proclaims that an illegal act may eventually acquire legal status if, as a matter of empirical fact, it is recognized on the international plane. Our law has long recognized that through a combination of acquiescence and prescription, an illegal act may at some later point be accorded some form of legal status. In the law of property, for example, it is well-known that a squatter on land may ultimately become the owner if the true owner sleeps on his or her right to repossess the land. In this way, a change in the factual circumstances may subsequently be reflected in a change in legal status. It is, however, quite another matter to suggest that a subsequent condonation of an initially illegal act retroactively creates a legal right to engage in the act in the first place. The broader contention is not supported by the international principle of effectivity or otherwise and must be rejected.

C. Question 3

In the event of a conflict between domestic and international law on the right of the National Assembly, legislature or government of Quebec to effect the secession of Quebec from Canada unilaterally, which would take precedence in Canada?

[147] In view of our answers to Questions 1 and 2, there is no conflict between domestic and international law to be addressed in the context of this Reference.

IV. Summary of Conclusions

[148] As stated at the outset, this Reference has required us to consider momentous questions that go to the heart of our system of constitutional government. We have emphasized that the Constitution is more than a written text. It embraces the entire global system of rules and principles which govern the exercise of constitutional authority. A superficial reading of selected provisions of the written constitutional enactment, without more, may be misleading. It is necessary to make a more profound investigation of the underlying principles that animate the whole of our Constitution, including the principles of federalism, democracy, constitutionalism and the rule of law, and respect for minorities. Those principles must inform our overall appreciation of the constitutional rights and obligations that would come into play in the event a clear majority of Quebecers votes on a clear question in favour of secession.

[149] The Reference requires us to consider whether Quebec has a right to *unilateral* secession. Those who support the existence of such a right found their case primarily on the principle of democracy. Democracy, however, means more than simple majority rule. As reflected in our constitutional jurisprudence, democracy exists in the larger context of other constitutional values such as those already mentioned. In the 131 years since Confederation, the people of the provinces and territories have created close ties of interdependence (economically, socially, politically and culturally) based on shared values that include federalism, democracy, constitutionalism and the rule of law, and respect for minorities. A democratic decision of Quebecers in favour of secession would put those relationships at risk. The Constitution vouchsafes order and stability, and accordingly secession of a province "under the Constitution" could not be achieved unilaterally, that is, without principled negotiation with other participants in Confederation within the existing constitutional framework.

[150] The Constitution is not a straitjacket. Even a brief review of our constitutional history demonstrates periods of momentous and dramatic change. Our democratic institutions necessarily accommodate a continuous process of discussion and evolution, which is reflected in the constitutional right of each participant in the federation to initiate constitutional change. This right implies a reciprocal duty on the other participants to engage in discussions to address any legitimate initiative to change the constitutional order. While it is

true that some attempts at constitutional amendment in recent years have faltered, a clear majority vote in Quebec on a clear question in favour of secession would confer democratic legitimacy on the secession initiative which all of the other participants in Confederation would have to recognize.

[151] Quebec could not, despite a clear referendum result, purport to invoke a right of self-determination to dictate the terms of a proposed secession to the other parties to the federation. The democratic vote, by however strong a majority, would have no legal effect on its own and could not push aside the principles of federalism and the rule of law, the rights of individuals and minorities, or the operation of democracy in the other provinces or in Canada as a whole. Democratic rights under the Constitution cannot be divorced from constitutional obligations. Nor, however, can the reverse proposition be accepted. The continued existence and operation of the Canadian constitutional order could not be indifferent to a clear expression of a clear majority of Quebecers that they no longer wish to remain in Canada. The other provinces and the federal government would have no basis to deny the right of the government of Quebec to pursue secession, should a clear majority of the people of Quebec choose that goal, so long as in doing so, Quebec respects the rights of others. The negotiations that followed such a vote would address the potential act of secession as well as its possible terms should in fact secession proceed. There would be no conclusions predetermined by law on any issue. Negotiations would need to address the interests of the other provinces, the federal government, Quebec and indeed the rights of all Canadians both within and outside Quebec, and specifically the rights of minorities. No one suggests that it would be an easy set of negotiations.

[152] The negotiation process would require the reconciliation of various rights and obligations by negotiation between two legitimate majorities, namely, the majority of the population of Quebec, and that of Canada as a whole. A political majority at either level that does not act in accordance with the underlying constitutional principles we have mentioned puts at risk the legitimacy of its exercise of its rights, and the ultimate acceptance of the result by the international community.

[153] The task of the Court has been to clarify the legal framework within which political decisions are to be taken "under the Constitution", not to usurp the prerogatives of the political forces that operate within that framework. The obligations we have identified are binding obligations under the Constitution of Canada. However, it will be for the political actors to determine what constitutes "a clear majority on a

clear question" in the circumstances under which a future referendum vote may be taken. Equally, in the event of demonstrated majority support for Quebec secession, the content and process of the negotiations will be for the political actors to settle. The reconciliation of the various legitimate constitutional interests is necessarily committed to the political rather than the judicial realm precisely because that reconciliation can only be achieved through the give and take of political negotiations. To the extent issues addressed in the course of negotiation are political, the courts, appreciating their proper role in the constitutional scheme, would have no supervisory role.

[154] We have also considered whether a positive legal entitlement to secession exists under international law in the factual circumstances contemplated by Question 1, i.e., a clear democratic expression of support on a clear question for Quebec secession. Some of those who supported an affirmative answer to this question did so on the basis of the recognized right to self-determination that belongs to all "peoples". Although much of the Quebec population certainly shares many of the characteristics of a people, it is not necessary to decide the "people" issue because, whatever may be the correct determination of this issue in the context of Quebec, a right to secession only arises under the principle of self-determination of peoples at international law where "a people" is governed as part of a colonial empire; where "a people" is subject to alien subjugation, domination or exploitation; and possibly where "a people" is denied any meaningful exercise of its right to self-determination within the state of which it forms a part. In other circumstances, peoples are expected to achieve self-determination within the framework of their existing state. A state whose government represents the whole of the people or peoples resident within its territory, on a basis of equality and without discrimination, and respects the principles of self-determination in its internal arrangements, is entitled to maintain its territorial integrity under international law and to have that territorial integrity recognized by other states. Quebec does not meet the threshold of a colonial people or an oppressed people, nor can it be suggested that Quebecers have been denied meaningful access to government to pursue their political, economic, cultural and social development. In the circumstances, the National Assembly, the legislature or the government of Quebec do not enjoy a right at international law to effect the secession of Quebec from Canada unilaterally.

[155] Although there is no right, under the Constitution or at international law, to unilateral secession, that is secession without negotiation on the basis just discussed, this does not rule out the possibility of

an unconstitutional declaration of secession leading to a *de facto* secession. The ultimate success of such a secession would be dependent on recognition by the international community, which is likely to consider the legality and legitimacy of secession having regard to, amongst other facts, the conduct of Quebec and Canada, in determining whether to grant or withhold recognition. Such recognition, even if granted, would not, however, provide any retroactive justification for the act of secession, either under the Constitution of Canada or at international law.

[156] The reference questions are answered accordingly.

The Attorney General's Vision

Jean Leclair
Translated by I.M. Milne

Jean Leclair teaches at the Faculty of Law, Université de Montréal. This article is abridged from "Impoverishment of the Law by the Law: A Critique of the Attorney General's Vision of the Rule of Law and the Federal Principle" in Constitutional Forum constitutionnel *10 (1998): 1-8.*

This brief article is devoted to a critique of the arguments put forward by the Attorney General of Canada in connection with the Reference concerning certain questions relating to the secession of Quebec. I will examine, in particular, how the approach taken by the Attorney General impoverished the legal concepts of the rule of law and federalism.

The position of the Attorney General of Canada as to the relevance of the concepts of the rule of law and of federalism can be summarized as follows.

The Constitution of Canada is the supreme law of the land, the source of all authority. It determines the extent and limits of the powers of both levels of government. Any standard that contravenes the Constitution can be declared legally invalid. Furthermore, the Constitution sanctions a principle already recognized in Canadian law, namely the rule of law, according to which, to prevent the arbitrary exercise of power, any action by the state must be authorized by law. Order and justice are therefore assured, as the state may act only in compliance with clear and previously stated rules that it has adopted itself. The courts are the guardians of the rule of law. Lastly, since Part V of the Constitution Act, 1982, expressly establishes the rules to be followed to amend the Constitution, it follows that it is the only applicable standard.

The Attorney General maintained that section 45 of the Constitution Act, 1982, the only one allowing a province unilaterally to amend a part of the Constitution, did not authorize secession; no one disputed this assertion. The issue, the Attorney General maintained, was therefore resolved. It followed, she said, that the Court did not have to make any further determination; the interpretation of section 45 sufficed. The Court did not have to "stray into" issues such as how secession might be effected, or express an opinion on the merits of the sovereignist project. It did not have to explain whether other principles could have been invoked in support of such a project. Neither did it have to express an opinion on the relevance of a national referendum, or on the need to obtain consent from the aboriginal peoples. She even seemed reluctant to allow that the provinces could make a political commitment to recognize the right of the people of Quebec to unilaterally decide their own future. For the Attorney General, the rule of law compelled the Court to limit its examination to section 45 of the Constitution.

The Attorney General also enlisted the federal principle in support of her case against a province's right to secede. She said, "[o]ne of the consequences of the federal principle in Canada is that no single governmental institution — whether at the central or provincial level — can claim plenary authority over the population of a given province," which naturally excluded the power of a province to become fully sovereign. While the Attorney General recognized that "there is a Quebec people in a sociological, historical and political sense," in her view Quebec nevertheless remained a province like the others: "a full and equal — indeed a founding — member of the federation. The legislature of Quebec, *like other provincial legislatures*, exercises numerous important heads of power and enjoys significant autonomy under Canada's federal constitutional structure [emphasis added]." Lastly, when the concept of federalism is put forward, the emphasis is oddly on unity and not diversity, as, for example, when the Supreme Court referred in *Morguard* to "the obvious intention of the Constitution [of 1867] to create a single country."

In short, we learn that the values of federalism and rule of law (and of democracy), "[f]ar from superseding or supplanting the terms of the Constitution, [...] are found in the Constitution's specific amending provisions and reinforce their application."

Pressed by the Court, which was anxious to know whether there were some principles that would show the way out of the deadlock brought about by the impossibility of obtaining the consent required by Part V to effect a secession, the Attorney General replied: "it is not Part V that would have 'failed' if a constitutional amendment proposal did not obtain the required resolutions of assent, but rather, the particular proposal under consideration." The Constitution triumphed absolutely. The *Titanic* was indeed unsinkable. The ship did not sink; the water level, unfortunately, rose above the upper decks ...

The preceding definitions of rule of law and federalism are perfectly consistent with what is found in most works of constitutional law. They are both deficient, however, in that they are based on the presumption that legal standards adopted by the state have an objectively identifiable content of universal scope. They conceal the fact that the porosity of these standards allows their interpreters to inflect their meaning. In this way, meaning becomes largely determined by the expectations of the target audience. Here comes into play the concept of legitimacy, which is not to be confused with strict adherence to a constitutional standard stripped of any context.

The political institutions of a given society and the laws that they pass will appear legitimate (in the sense that the people will freely agree to obey them) to the extent that such institutions are in tune with the values and beliefs of the community members. Legitimacy thus presupposes the possibility of dialogue amongst the various segments of the community and between state institutions and those segments. A political (or even judicial) institution that fails to defend concepts of humanity, of community and of public interest in keeping with people's expectations will see its legitimacy and its power to constrain start to dwindle. These values will, among other things, constitute the horizon, the background of intelligibility, used by the judges as a basis for interpreting the vague concepts expressed above. The interpretation of these concepts, which in their abstract form appear universal, will be sustained by "local" values.

It is from this point of view that the concepts of the rule of law and federalism must be considered.

Faithfulness to the law, even constitutional law, is not necessarily identical with faithfulness to the moral ideal, to the aspiration that underlies the notion of the rule of law. Strict adherence to official legality may be nothing more than faithfulness to a legality stripped of any ethical concerns. I agree with Jeremy Webber's view that the rule of law means that the exercise of any political power is linked to an obligation to justify political actions in the eyes of all.[1] All political power must aim at the common interest ahead of special interests; a political action is therefore justified only if it tends to promote a concept of the public interest that can be defended publicly, before society *as a whole*. Such a power will be legitimate insofar as, within such a context, the decisions made by political institutions appear acceptable, even to those who oppose them.

The Attorney General's description of the federal principle was disarmingly simplistic. Federalism in fact represents much more than a simple method of distributing powers between levels of government. Were the federal principle merely an abstract concept, there would be no difference between Belgian, Swiss, U.S. and Canadian federalism. However, no constitutional theory that takes history into account, nor any moral vision of what Canadian federalism might signify, enlivened the Attorney General's dry description. It was therefore impossible for the judges to determine, from such a definition, what gives Canadian federalism its particular texture. Before choices can be meaningful, those things which sustain such choices must be made manifest. This lack of vision was distressing for everyone, not just for Quebec.

The current crisis in Canada fits into a historical continuity. History can therefore not be ignored without trivializing the Canadian constitutional conflict.

Unlike the situation in the United States, nationhood has never been taken for granted in Canada. It is always in the process of being built. I agree with Samuel LaSelva's assertion that Canadian nationality presupposes Canadian federalism, which in turn rests on a complex form of fraternity between diverse communities — this fraternity being directed as much toward those who share our way of life as it is toward those who have adopted alternative ways of life.[2] This concept of fraternity, not being totally disembodied, recognizes the tragic failures of this brotherhood (the tragic fate of the aboriginal peoples and of francophones outside Quebec) and recognizes the greatness as well as the poverty of the Canadian federal structure. However, in the final analysis, if Canada is to survive, it is because some people are convinced that the acceptance of differences is the royal road to a more just society.

Canadian federalism is therefore based on a mutual recognition of differences — meaningful differences, that is, for they are not all equal. A thing does not necessarily become important simply because it is asserted. It becomes so when this choice fits into a particular *shared* horizon of significance allowing agreement on the importance of a given difference. While it is self-evident that each province is distinct in its own way, the provinces do not all display such a degree of specificity as to justify creating distinctions among them, if we are to be guided by the fundamental characteristic of Canadian federalism as it evolved from 1867, namely, the existence of a Quebec in which the majority language and culture is French. Any definition of Canadian federalism that ignores Quebec's (and aboriginal peoples') distinctiveness will never be legitimate. By fiercely trying not to look at the past (and even at the present), and by clinging solely to defining abstract legal norms which in themselves have no ontological significance, we deprive ourselves of the power to make valid choices and to give meaning to law, which is anything but trivial and which can, on the contrary, engender legitimacy.

If all reference to the horizon of significance that history represents is eliminated, then all choices are equally valid, all equally important, and the net result is an anemic, trivial and even absurd version of Canadian federalism.

The Arguments of the
Amicus Curiae

Bruce Ryder

Bruce Ryder teaches at Osgoode Hall Law School, York University. This essay is abridged from "A Court in Need and a Friend Indeed: An Analysis of the Arguments of the Amicus Curiae *in the Quebec Secession Reference." in* Constitutional Forum constitutionnel *10 (1998): 9-13.*

The *amicus curiae* took on a daunting challenge in assuming the task assigned to him by the Supreme Court of Canada in the Quebec Secession Reference. In agreeing to fill the gap left by the absence of the Quebec government from the proceedings, and in presenting arguments opposed to the positions taken by the Attorney General of Canada, Maître André Joli-Coeur had a legal deck stacked against him. The federal government framed the reference questions in such a way as to minimize the risk that it would get answers that it did not like. The questions were aimed directly at the legal Achilles heel of the sovereignty movement, namely, that their project prior to and following the 1995 referendum had relied ultimately on the possibility of pursuing a unilateral declaration of independence, a rupture of the Canadian constitutional order.

The vast majority of legal scholars agree that Quebec has no right to unilateral secession in domestic or international law.[1] It came as no surprise, then, that the Supreme Court's opinion in the Secession Reference dismissed all of the *amicus*'s arguments in short order. What is perhaps more surprising is that the authority of the Supreme Court's opinion was nevertheless quickly accepted by the government of Quebec. Many of the arguments put forward by the *amicus* had formed the basis of the Quebec government's refusal to partici- pate in the proceedings. Similarly, the *amicus* presented the same arguments used by sovereignists to portray the unilateral path to sovereignty as legitimate and ultimately lawful.

In this comment, I will briefly canvass the *amicus's* arguments and the Supreme Court's response to them. Then I will explore how the Supreme Court was able to bring sovereignists into a conversa- tion framed by its opinion, at the same time as it was pulling the legal rug they had previously relied upon out from underneath them.

On the distinctly unfriendly legal terrain presented by the Refer- ence questions, the "friend of the court" pursued two basic strategies in his submissions.

The first strategy was to argue that the Supreme Court should not answer the questions. Maître Joli-Coeur argued that the Court should refuse to issue an opinion because the questions were too theoretical, too political, too hypothetical, were concerned solely with interna- tional law, and, in any case, federal and provincial laws conferring the power to hear references on the Supreme Court and provincial courts of appeal, respectively, are unconstitutional....

Maître Joli-Coeur's second strategy for avoiding a contest he could not win was to answer different questions than those presented to the Court. Instead of pressing the argument that Quebec has a *right* of unilateral secession, and the federal government a corresponding obligation to facilitate the exercise of that right, Maître Joli-Coeur's submissions stayed for the most part on firmer ground. He argued that a legally effective unilateral secession is possible and is not prohibited by international law. He conceded that the international right of all peoples to self-determination did not give the Quebec people a right to secede. However, he argued, the unilateral estab- lishment of a sovereign Quebec state will be recognized at interna- tional law if Quebec can establish effective control over its territory. Domestic constitutional law, he said, eventually would have to yield to the reality of an effectively sovereign Quebec state. When pushed, in questioning from the Court, to reveal details of his position — for example, how this principle of effectivity would operate, and how it would deal with the competing rights of self-determination of the multiple peoples within Quebec (and Canada) — Maître Joli-Coeur reverted to his first strategy (as counsel for the Attorney General of Canada did in response to similarly difficult questions directed to him): the Court's questions were too hypothetical, too political, or beyond the Court's jurisdiction.

The heart of the *amicus*'s submissions can be summarized as follows: Quebec may proceed unilaterally to accomplish the secession of Quebec from Canada by virtue of the principle of effectivity. A secession will be effective when the government of Quebec exercises all state authority over the territory of Quebec. The establishment of effective and exclusive sovereignty will be founded on the democratic legitimacy of a majority vote of the Québécois people exercising their right of self-determination. Maître Joli-Coeur's arguments were not novel or unusual in this regard; the principle of effectivity has been suggested as the legal basis of Quebec's accession to sovereignty by a range of scholars. Frémont and Boudreault, for example, have argued that the Canadian Constitution does not apply to secession and thus Quebec "serait alors lui-même condamné à procéder à sa propre révolution."[2] Like the *amicus curiae*'s submissions, sovereignist scholarship in recent years has shifted from reliance on a right of self-determination to reliance on the alleged legitimacy and eventual legality of an effective assertion of sovereignty.

The view that a unilateral secession can lead ultimately to the establishment of a new sovereign state recognized by other members of the international community is as uncontroversial as the federal government's position that a unilateral process would amount to an illegal rupture of Canadian constitutional continuity. Should the Quebec government and people choose to pursue the unilateral path to sovereignty, however, we are all in for a perilous journey. If Quebec were to follow the *amicus*'s approach and attempt to assert effective control to achieve international recognition of an illegal secession, and if the federal government were to continue to take the position that it has an obligation to uphold the existing constitutional order until a negotiated settlement is reached, then the spectre of civil disorder and violence would loom large. The failure to even acknowledge the risk of such disastrous consequences accompanying a unilateral secession was the most troubling aspect of the *amicus*'s submissions.

Moreover, the reliance on the principle of effectivity raises a host of practical and theoretical problems, some of them highlighted in the written questions members of the Court directed at the *amicus*. One basic problem is that the principle of effectivity will come into operation only when the government of Canada has ceased to exercise sovereign authority in Quebec. When asked by the Court how, when and according to what principles the federal government should or must withdraw, the *amicus* had nothing to say (other than that the question itself is beyond the jurisdiction of the Court). This question highlights the difference between unilateral secession as an initially illegal course of action that might become legally effective if a new regime can exercise exclusive sovereignty, and unilateral secession as a *right* that the government of Canada is *obliged* to respect. As Professor Crawford stated in his reply to the *amicus*'s experts, "international law permits the metropolitan state to oppose [secession] by all means consistent with non-derogable human rights and humanitarian law, permits the conduct [of secessionists] to be classified as criminal, and prohibits other states from providing any material assistance to [the secessionists]."[3] Moreover, the Attorney General of Canada took the position before the Court that the federal government has an obligation to ensure respect for the existing constitution. Unless the government of Canada changes its position, the principle of effectivity would only come into play if the exercise of Canadian sovereignty is ended by the use of force.

Another basic question raised by the *amicus*'s position is whether *any* group can rely on the principle of effectivity to secede unilaterally from an established state such as Canada (or a future sovereign Quebec, for that matter). How does the principle espoused by Maître Joli-Coeur contain such anarchic possibilities?

Maître Joli-Coeur did not rely on the principle of effective control alone. He implicitly acknowledged that some secessionist attempts at establishing control through revolutionary means are worthy of respect and others properly resisted by the state. In Quebec's case, he argued that the assertion of effective control would be legitimized by the Québécois people's expression through democratic means of their right of self-determination. In other words, recourse to the principle of effectivity is particularly legitimate when a people has exercised its right of self-determination by putting its political future to a democratic vote. Maître Joli-Coeur conceded that the right of self-determination cannot be equated, in Quebec's case, to a right to secede. But, he seemed to suggest, the right of self-determination may provide moral and political legitimacy to any attempt to assert effective control if secession is the choice of the people. In that sense, he says, the exercise of the right of self-determination by "le peuple québécois fait partie du processus de la sécession éventuelle du Québec."

This position begs an important question: who exactly is "le peuple québécois"? Is there a single people within the province of Quebec? In the *amicus*'s submissions, as in political discourse in Quebec more generally, there is considerable slippage between civic and ethnic understandings of the Quebec people. That is, sometimes "le peuple québécois" includes all persons living in the province, at other times it seems to include only Quebecers who are of French-Canadian heritage. Pressed to clarify his position on this issue by the Court, Maître Joli-Coeur conceded that there is not a single people living in Quebec. To his credit, and in contrast to the official Parti Québécois position, he said that the eleven aboriginal nations in Quebec have the same rights as "le peuple québécois" to unilateral secession relying on the principle of effectivity as an expression of their right of self-determination.

Further, when asked if there is a Canadian people, Maître Joli-Coeur took the uncontrovertible position that there is no single Canadian people. Rather, he said, there is at least an English-Canadian people, a Québécois people, aboriginal peoples, and an Acadian people. He acknowledged that all peoples have recourse to the same rights at international law. According to the *amicus*'s own logic then, aboriginal peoples and representatives of the English-Canadian people within Quebec may choose to exercise their democratic right to stay in Canada. The principle of effectivity, when it draws its legitimacy from a people's exercise of the right of self-determination, leads directly to partitionist scenarios given that Quebec, like the rest of Canada, is a multinational society.

Therefore, far from being compatible with the rule of law, as the *amicus* contended, reliance on the principle of effectivity as the sole legal norm relevant to the achievement of sovereignty leads to a situation where we would have two competing regimes, one legal and constitutional, the other illegal and unconstitutional, both claiming authority over the same territory and peoples, both with passionate supporters relying on the exercise of their right to self-determination and the view that international law eventually will recognize the victor in the struggle for effective control. This is a scenario fraught with risks of social, economic and political disorder.

In the light of these difficulties, it came as no surprise that the Supreme Court rejected the proposition that the principle of effectivity gives rise to a legal right to unilateral secession. The principle of effectivity, the judges said, "proclaims that an illegal act may eventually acquire legal status if, as a matter of empirical fact, it is recognized on the international plane." However, the subsequent condonation of an illegal act does not "retroactively create a legal right to engage in the act in the first place" (para. 146). The Court commented that while unilateral secession would therefore be initially illegal according to both domestic and international law, "this does not rule out the possibility of an unconstitutional declaration of secession leading to a *de facto* secession" (para. 155)....

Maître Joli-Coeur struggled valiantly to make legal arguments to support a position contrary to that taken by the Attorney General of Canada in the Secession Reference. His submissions, however, accomplished only one thing: they revealed the weakness of the best available arguments in support of a legal right to unilateral secession. In this sense, the *amicus* proved to be a friend of the Court indeed. His contributions lent greater authority to the Court's rejection of the legal arguments that had previously undergirded the unilateral component of sovereignist strategy leading up to the 1995 referendum. The defective legal underpinnings of this strategy have now been effectively exposed, and the debate has shifted to the threshold conditions that would have to be met before a duty to negotiate secession in good faith arises. The justices should be applauded for crafting an opinion that seeks to minimize the risks of social disorder that would accompany any unilateral declaration of sovereignty and to maximize the chances of a negotiated, peaceful accommodation of the political aspirations of a clear majority of Quebecers clearly expressed in any future referendum.

The Aboriginal Argument: the Requirement of Aboriginal Consent

Andrew Orkin and Joanna Birenbaum

Andrew Orkin, of the Ontario Bar, was part of the legal team acting on behalf of the Grand Council of the Crees in the Quebec Secession Reference. Joanna Birenbaum is also of the Ontario Bar.

Aboriginal peoples are the "most vulnerable [to] and most affected" by the secessionist aspirations and threats of the province of Quebec, according to Supreme Court of Canada Justice Peter Cory. Both in oral statements and in the Quebec Secession Reference, the Court acknowledged "the importance" of the submissions made to it by the aboriginal interveners "respecting the rights and concerns of aboriginal peoples in the event of a unilateral secession" (para. 139).

Yet, although it recognized the profound impact of secession on the rights and interests of aboriginal peoples, the Court held that it was unnecessary for it to rule directly on the aboriginal concerns and arguments raised. Unfortunately, this exercise of judicial restraint meant that in addition to leaving these questions for another day, the primary argument presented by the aboriginal interveners, which can be summarized as "no secession without our consent," was not made available to the public by way of the judgement of the Court. Nor did the public gain full exposure to the depth and breadth of the claims made by aboriginal peoples in the Quebec Secession case.

This brief essay, therefore, is an opportunity to present a summary of the facts and legal arguments in support of the claim that Quebec secession can only be lawfully achieved under domestic or international law with the full participation and consent of the affected aboriginal peoples. It is also an opportunity to reflect on the decision of the Supreme Court of Canada in the Quebec Secession Reference in the light of the arguments put to it by the aboriginal interveners.[1]

The Requirement of Consent

The Court justified its exercise of judicial restraint regarding the arguments raised by aboriginal peoples by stating that "the concern of aboriginal peoples is precipitated by the asserted right of Quebec to unilateral secession." In finding that Quebec has no such right, the Court went on to argue that, as "aboriginal interests would be taken into account," in the constitutional negotiations following a vote in support of secession, "it becomes unnecessary to explore further the concerns of aboriginal peoples in this Reference" (para. 139).

The Court in this paragraph, however, takes the aboriginal intervener arguments perhaps too literally. Although the aboriginal submissions (and those of all other parties) were directed by the Reference questions to the issue of unilateral secession, the cause that "precipitated" the concern of aboriginal peoples was not limited to the right of Quebec to secede unilaterally but was, more fundamentally, the prospect of secession altogether — *unilaterally or by any other means*. The principles developed in the argument giving rise to a legal requirement of aboriginal consent applied equally to any removal of aboriginal peoples or their territories from Canada. Put simply, the requirement of consent developed in the argument held that *no* formula or framework for achieving the secession of Quebec could be lawful or legitimate without the full participation and consent of aboriginal peoples.

The legal and factual bases for the requirement of aboriginal consent include:

1. the right of aboriginal peoples to self-determination;
2. treaty rights, in particular those arising from the the James Bay and Northern Quebec Agreement (JBNQA);
3. section 35 of the *Constitution Act, 1982*;
4. fiduciary relationships with the Crown;
5. a constitutional convention of consent;
6. the federal principle;
7. the democratic principle and other fundamental principles of human rights.

The Right to Self-Determination

All of the aboriginal interveners argued that the right to self-determination is a fundamental universal human right guaranteed by international human rights instruments,[2] and which applies to them as distinct "peoples" within Canada. Section 35 of the *Constitution Act, 1982*, recognizes aboriginal peoples as "peoples" without qualification. The Quebec National Assembly expressly recognizes aboriginal peoples in Quebec as distinct "nations." Internationally, the very existence of the Draft Declaration on the Rights of Indigenous Peoples indicates that indigenous peoples are recognized as "peoples" and not simply "minorities" under international law. Perhaps more importantly, the government of Canada has formally declared before the United Nations Commission on Human Rights that it "accepts a right to self-determination for indigenous peoples which respects the political, constitutional and territorial integrity of democratic States" and is "legal and morally committed to the observance and protection of this right."

As argued by the interveners and affirmed by the Court, the right to self-determination generally protects *internal* self-determination, that is the self-determination of peoples *within* existing states to freely determine their political status and pursue their economic, social and cultural development (paras. 118–119). The Court agreed with the aboriginal interveners that a right to external self-determination, which can include a right to secede, may arise where a people "is blocked from the meaningful exercise of its rights to self-determination internally" (para. 134). In the event of the forcible inclusion of aboriginal peoples into an independent Quebec, this exception may become relevant.

Treaty Rights

Through the JBNQA, the governments of Canada and Quebec entered into a treaty relationship with the two aboriginal parties, the James Bay Crees and the Nunavik Inuit. The treaty provides for the obligations of both governments to continue indefinitely in a federal arrangement under the Constitution. As pointed out by both the Cree and Inuit, the treaty was signed by the aboriginal parties on the specific understanding that they would have the benefit of dealing with two levels of government, with the federal government retaining a permanent and distinct fiduciary responsibility. An independent

Quebec would be fundamentally incompatible with the existing constitutional and legal arrangements under the Agreement.

Every chapter of the Agreement is subject to a general consent provision or else specifically includes a requirement for the consent of the Cree or Inuit party to any amendment or modification of the treaty. Under the Agreement, therefore, consent must be obtained from the aboriginal parties for any withdrawal from or transfer of governmental obligations under the treaty and any other proposal that would affect the treaty rights of the Inuit or Cree peoples. Such rights include assurances that the aboriginal parties will retain forever all of the rights of Canadian citizens generally, and the right to continued federal involvement in numerous aspects of the administration of Cree community territory and the James Bay Territory as a whole.

Section 35(1) of the *Constitution Act, 1982*

Section 35 of the *Constitution Act, 1982*, guarantees the treaty rights arising from the JBNQA, including the provisions concerning amendment and consent. The requirement of consent under the Agreement, therefore, becomes a constitutional requirement that the consent of the Cree and Inuit be obtained before their rights under the treaty are amended or modified.

Further, the Grand Council of the Crees argued that even had the JBNQA not contained specific consent provisions, one of the purposes of section 35(1) is "to provide an ongoing amendment procedure that confers constitutional protection on treaty rights, whenever acquired or modified."[3] Unilateral secession by Quebec or a negotiated secession without aboriginal consent would, therefore, be a fundamental breach of the Agreement, in contravention of the section 35(1) amending formula.

Fiduciary Relationship

As argued by the Crees and Inuit, the federal government, Parliament and the National Assembly or government of Quebec have fiduciary relationships with aboriginal peoples that impose constraints on the powers and rights of these governments and legislatures in the secession context. Moreover, these fiduciary relationships create fiduciary obligations of a constitutional nature, arising from the JBNQA, the legislation enacted pursuant to it, and section 35 of the *Constitution Act, 1982*. Other constitutional instruments, such as the *Royal Proclamation of 1763* and the *Rupert's Land and North-West Territory Order,* impose ongoing constitutional duties on at least the government of Canada and Parliament to act in a manner consistent with their fiduciary obligations.

In the context of the secession of Quebec, these fiduciary duties, the Crees and Inuit argued, "could only be carried out by respecting the wishes of Aboriginal peoples and the principle of Aboriginal consent" and would have to be interpreted "in a manner consistent with the constitutional requirement of obtaining Cree and Inuit consent to any modifications of their Treaty rights."

Constitutional Convention

Constitutional conventions are an integral part of the constitutional system and, when they are established, form part of the "Constitution." A constitutional convention is a binding non-legal rule that is created when the following three conditions are met: there is a precedent for the convention, the actors believe themselves to be bound by the rule and there is a good reason for the rule.

The Crees assert that there is now a constitutional convention in Canada that aboriginal consent is required for any constitutional amendments that would alter the rights of aboriginal peoples. In support of this position, they cite section 35.1 of the *Constitution Act, 1982* (convening a constitutional conference and inviting aboriginal peoples to participate, should amendments be proposed to constitutional provisions referring to them) and the draft legal text of the Charlottetown Accord, which proposed adding section 45.1 to the Constitution, requiring the substantial consent of aboriginal peoples before an amendment can be made to the Constitution that "directly refers to, or that amends a provision that directly refers to, one or more of the Aboriginal peoples of Canada or their governments." The Crees were able to cite constitutional scholars in support of the existence of this convention.[4]

The Federal Principle

The Court held the "federal principle" to be one of the underlying principles that "inform and sustain the constitutional text" (para. 49). In its response to the factum of the *amicus curiae,* the Grand Council of the Crees submitted that aboriginal peoples are constituent elements of the federal principle.

As one of three orders of government in Canada, the consent of aboriginal peoples would be required in any matter directly and fundamentally affecting their rights and interests. As well, aboriginal peoples would be full parties to any negotiations concerning the secession of Quebec.

The Democratic Principle

The democratic principle, another principle underlying the Constitution, is an essential principle relied upon by the government of Quebec in asserting its right to unilateral secession from Canada. According to the claims of secessionist Quebecers, an affirmative vote in a provincial referendum would confer democratic legitimacy on a unilateral declaration of independence.

Such a majority vote, however, undermines the expression of the democratic will of aboriginal peoples. Just prior to the 30 October 1995 referendum held by the government of Quebec, the James Bay Cree Nation, the Inuit of Nunavik and five Innu (Montagnais) communities each held their own referendums on 24, 25 and 26 October 1995 respectively. In these referendums, each of the aboriginal peoples overwhelmingly rejected (over 95%) being separated from Canada without their consent. The forcible inclusion of these aboriginal peoples into an independent Quebec on the basis of a majority vote in a province-wide referendum subverts the democratic principle upon which the legitimacy of such a referendum lies.

Respect for Fundamental Human Rights

Finally, throughout the arguments of the Grand Council of the Crees and the Makivik Corporation is a reminder to the Court that the history of the original inclusion of the James Bay Cree and Nunavik Inuit homelands into Canada without their knowledge, participation or consent cannot be repeated in modern times.

A misconception that pervades the secession debate is that the current boundaries of the province of Quebec represent the territory of Quebec upon entering into Confederation in 1867 and ought to be the territory with which Quebec would leave. In fact, the northern two-thirds of the present province of Quebec was annexed to the province through legislation in 1898 and 1912 without the participation and consent of the Cree, Inuit and other aboriginal peoples in these territories. The aboriginal peoples were thus seen at the time as essentially chattels which "passed with the land."

Any inclusion today of aboriginal territories into an independent Quebec or change to the JBNQA treaty arrangements without aboriginal consent would constitute an offensive act of neocolonialism and a grave violation of all of the constitutional norms, treaty rights and fiduciary duties discussed above, as well as of fundamental human rights under domestic and international law.

The Court's Decision from the Perspective of Aboriginal Rights

In answering the Reference questions put to it, the Court not only ruled that Quebec had no right to unilateral secession under Canadian or international law, but went further and laid down the legal ground rules governing Quebec's pursuit of secession. Relying on the dictates of the four principles that underlie and animate the Constitution — democracy, federalism, constitutionalism and the rule of law, and protection of minorities — the Court sketched the outlines of a constitutionally acceptable process for secession.

The most troubling aspect of the Court's ruling from an aboriginal perspective is its failure to explicitly recognize the heightened and binding constitutional rights of aboriginal peoples in the context of secession. Once the Court took it upon itself to formulate a broad framework for a legal and legitimate process of secession, the binding and non-negotiable aboriginal rights which would form part of and constrain such a process should have been acknowledged.

While the Court saw fit to rule well beyond the three Reference questions by formulating a legally acceptable framework for secession, it did not see fit to do so in any detail with respect to some of the concerns brought to it by aboriginal peoples. Disappointingly, the opportunity to provide clarity concerning the rights of the acknowledgedly most vulnerable affected parties was not fully seized at this time.

First, while in no way excluding the possibility, the Court did not specifically identify the affected aboriginal peoples as "parties" to the negotiation process. The "parties" to the negotiation process appear to be defined as the "parties to Confederation." Under the federalism principle, a repudiation of the existing constitutional order by a province "gives rise to a reciprocal obligation on all parties to Confederation to negotiate constitutional changes to respond to that desire" (para. 88). In its exploration of the history of Confederation, the Court omitted explicit mention of aboriginal peoples and of their treaty relationships with the Crown, which this Court has confirmed in other judgements, and which are an essential part of this history and our current constitutional structure (see *R. v. Van der Peet* [1996] and *Delgamuukw v. British Columbia* [1997]).

Second, the apparent flexibility of the amending process and the language of balancing or "reconciliation" of rights and interests is inconsistent with the JBNQA and section 35(1) of the Constitution. While it may be generally true that in the context of secession the "rights, obligations and legitimate aspirations of all Canadians" (which presumably in law also includes aboriginal peoples in Canada) have to be reconciled, this balancing of rights cannot justify constitutional arrangements that impact on the treaty and other rights of aboriginal peoples without their consent. The Court's decision not to make this constitutional requirement explicit, and then additionally to imply that aboriginal rights can be approached within a framework of balancing of rights, undermines the allegedly equal weight the Court attributes to the principle of the protection of aboriginal peoples. It also fails to take seriously the special constitutional status of aboriginal peoples under Part II of the *Constitution Act, 1982*.

Another related and somewhat troubling aspect of the decision is the fact that the only place where the rights of aboriginal peoples are considered directly by the Court is in its discussion of the principle of "protection of minorities." In contrast, the Court omitted the rights of aboriginal peoples from its discussion of the principles of democracy and federalism. Aboriginal peoples did present themselves to the Court as entities entitled to protection under the Constitution. However, they did so primarily as one of three orders of government within the federal principle; this particular status, they asserted, arises from their standing as self-determining nations whose nation-to-nation and treaty relationships with the Crown are part of the very building-blocks of Canada. Read in isolation, the apparent fitting of the rights of aboriginal peoples into only the principle of "protection of minorities" in the context of secession creates an impression of paternalism, and cannot be seen as overruling the Court's other rulings that aboriginal peoples are distinct and separate from "minority groups" in Canada (see again *Van der Peet* and *Delamuukw, supra*).

Finally, the Court in a number of places in the decision slips into somewhat regressive usage (which, again taken in isolation, is inconsistent with its other decisions). For example, at the same time as recognizing the territorial claims of aboriginal peoples, the Court may have inadvertently diminished them by stating that the issue of the boundaries of a seceding Quebec would have to be on the table and would include "a regard for the northern lands occupied largely by aboriginal peoples" (para. 139). The northern lands of Quebec are not just "occupied" by aboriginal peoples, but are subject to extensive and constitutionally entrenched treaty rights in their favour. As the importance of these treaty rights has been recognized by the Court in other decisions, it is unclear why such language was used in this ruling. Presumably the Court did not intend that respect for the requirements of Part II of the Constitution Act, 1982, would require that only "a regard" be paid to these concerns.

Similarly, despite recognizing, at a minimum, the constitutional value of the protection of aboriginal peoples and the "ancient occupation of the land by aboriginal peoples" (para. 82), the Court defines negotiation of secession as requiring the "reconciliation of various rights and obligations by the representatives of *two legitimate majorities,* namely, the clear majority of the population of Quebec and the clear majority of Canada as a whole, whatever that may be" (para. 93, emphasis added). What does this statement mean for aboriginal peoples, and where do aboriginal peoples fit in this framework? Moreover, why was the distinct status of aboriginal peoples as *legitimate majorities in their own right* in the context of secession apparently ignored by the Court?

Notwithstanding the above criticisms and concerns, the Court does make a number of highly significant statements in its decision that further entrench and protect aboriginal rights in Canada. This makes the ruling a victory for aboriginal peoples. For example, the interveners' fundamental position that their territories could not simply be assumed to "pass" with a seceding Quebec was vindicated by the Court's unequivocal statements that put the question of the boundaries of a seceding Quebec on the negotiating table (para. 139). Perhaps the most important aspect of the decision for aboriginal peoples is the Supreme Court's recognition, for the first time, of the right to self-determination as a "general principle of international law" (para. 114) that is applicable within Canada. Accordingly, aboriginal peoples can now continue to forcefully advance their rights to self-determination under Canadian law and specifically to assert a right to full participation and informed consent in the context of Quebec secession. As well, the Court's recognition of the right to external self-determination in exceptional circumstances adds leverage and legal legitimacy to any expression by aboriginal peoples in Quebec of their desire to maintain and strengthen their nation-to-nation relationship with Canada in the face of efforts by other political actors purporting to deal with their territories in direct conflict with this expressed will.

4

Prime Minister Jean Chrétien's Response

Jean Chrétien

This is the text of a speech delivered by Prime Minister Jean Chrétien on 21 August 1998.

The ruling yesterday by the Supreme Court of Canada is of extraordinary importance. It is not a victory for governments or politicians. It is a victory for all Canadians. It protects the legal and democratic rights of citizens of our country for the future.

It establishes the legal framework in which democratic decisions are to be taken. It sets out clearly the principles under which Canada has grown and flourished: federalism, democracy, constitutionalism and the rule of law, and respect for minorities.

There has been a lot of comment in the last twenty-four hours about yesterday's Supreme Court decision. Let me summarize briefly the most important elements of the decision:

1. The unilateral declaration of independence which the current Quebec government had in its back pocket before the last referendum is contrary to Canadian law and to the fundamental principles of democracy.
2. Such a unilateral declaration of independence is not supported by international law. So much then for one of the principal myths the advocates of separation have tried to create over the years.
3. Secession is as much a legal act as a political act.
4. The legal framework in which democratic decisions are to be taken includes the rights and obligations of Canadians who live

outside the Province of Quebec as well as those who live within Quebec. In particular, the rights of other provinces and specifically the rights of minorities.

5. This is very important. And I quote: "The referendum result, if it is to be taken as an expression of the democratic will, must be free of ambiguity, both in terms of the question asked and in terms of the support it generates."

6. This means that the days of the "*astuces*" of Mr. Parizeau and the "winning questions" of Mr. Bouchard are over. For a referendum to have any legitimacy, the question must be clear. And by clear, the Supreme Court does not refer to a question on some vague notion of partnership like the "winning" question of 1995. The Court refers specifically to the need for a question that provides, and I quote: "the clear expression of a clear majority of Quebecers that they no longer wish to remain in Canada."

7. The Supreme Court of Canada speaks of the need for an "enhanced majority" in order to alter the fundamental balances of political power. In other words, the secession of a province is so fundamental that it requires more than a simple majority for the results of a referendum question on secession to have any legitimacy. According to the Court, there must be no ambiguity in the result.

8. The Court also tells us that democracy requires a good-faith negotiation where a clear majority of Quebecers clearly express that they no longer want to be part of Canada. Not being part of Canada is not a sovereignty-partnership. It is not a sovereignty-association. It is secession. I quote, again, from the Court: "A clear majority on a clear question in favour of secession." That is the position which was advocated by the lawyers for the federal government before the Supreme Court of Canada.

9. In such a case, the Court indicates the complexity and difficulty of the negotiations and suggests that everything would be on the table. This includes the division of the national debt, boundaries, the protection of linguistic and cultural minorities, the rights of aboriginal people amongst others.

10. Accordingly, the Court says that "Nobody seriously suggests that our national existence, seamless in so many aspects, could be effortlessly separated along the now provincial boundaries of Quebec."

But our objective is not to spend our time talking about how this country could break up.

Our objective is to continue to build a strong, united country, respectful of the rights and obligations, the hopes and dreams of all its citizens.

A country that is economically prosperous and socially just.

A country that respects minorities.

A country of two official languages.

A country with a thriving French culture, centred in Quebec.

A country which welcomes citizens from all over the world.

Twice in less than a generation, despite ambiguous questions, the people of Quebec have chosen to be part of all of Canada.

And Canadians outside of Quebec have expressed in countless ways their desire for the Quebec society, with its unique character, to remain an essential part of Canada.

As we go forward, our task is to ensure that there be no more referendums on dismantling Canada. Rather, we must devote all our energies to building Canada in a way that Quebecers can focus on the wonderful opportunities of being full participants in Canada.

5

Premier Lucien Bouchard Reflects on the Ruling

Lucien Bouchard

Premier Lucien Bouchard delivered this statement in Quebec City on 21 August 1998.

An important political event took place yesterday, the effects of which we have not yet finished assessing.

With the scarcely concealed aim of raising fear among Quebecers, the federal government unilaterally asked nine judges of its own Supreme Court, nine persons whose federalist faith is not in doubt, to pronounce themselves on the Canadian federalist arguments.

The Quebec government, in keeping with its responsibility, refused to participate in this episode of the federal political strategy, and firmly reiterated that only the citizens of Quebec have the right to choose their future, as has moreover been stated by all parties represented in the National Assembly.

Yesterday's event thus embodied the Canadian government's attempt to have its own Court and its own judges validate the central elements of its Plan B, its anti-sovereignist offensive.

What happened was the reverse: the Court demonstrated that Ottawa's arguments do not stand up to analysis, and it struck at the very heart of the traditional federalist discourse.

Overall, the federalists have been telling us for the past two years that sovereignty is a legal issue that comes within the realm of law and the court system. The federal judges contradicted them. After having answered the reductionist questions asked by the federal government, in a perfectly foreseen and predictable manner, the

Court affirmed, from one end of its opinion to the other, the political nature of the process that would legitimately be set in motion by a Quebec referendum on sovereignty.

Allow me to peruse, one by one, the federalist myths that were buried yesterday by the federal judges.

First myth: for decades, a certain number of federalists have contended that the sovereignist project is not legitimate.

The judges of the Supreme Court stated the contrary, "A clear majority vote in Quebec on a clear question in favour of secession would confer democratic legitimacy on the secession initiative which all of the other participants in Confederation would have to recognize."

They go even further to state, "The other provinces and the federal government would have no basis to deny the right of the government of Quebec to pursue secession."

The federal judges thus upheld what sovereignists have been saying for thirty years: not only will a winning referendum have democratic legitimacy, but also Canada will have the obligation to recognize this legitimacy, and will not be able to deny Quebec the right to achieve sovereignty.

Second myth: in 1980 and in 1995, the federalists claimed that if the citizens of Quebec said Yes, Canada would refuse to negotiate with the government of Quebec. It will be recalled that in 1980, Mr. Pierre Trudeau compared the will of Quebecers to negotiate to that of a third-world country that Ottawa would not have to take into account. Again in 1995, the federalist advocates ridiculed the hand held out by the sovereignists for a negotiation after a Yes vote.

On October 12, 1995, Mr. Jean Chrétien made the following statement: "there is a myth that must be destroyed," he said, "to the effect that there is someone in Canada who is authorized to negotiate" with Quebec. The current leader of the Liberal Party of Quebec also made a few unfortunate statements on this subject.

Yesterday, unanimously, the federal judges brought to an end what had constituted the most fallacious argument of the federalist camp. The federal judges stated and restated that after a Yes vote, Canada would have the obligation to negotiate with Quebec. They even make this a constitutional obligation.

Allow me to quote a passage which reads as follows: "The clear repudiation by the people of Quebec of the existing constitutional order would confer legitimacy on demands for secession, and place an obligation on the other provinces and the federal government to acknowledge and respect that expression of democratic will by entering into negotiations [...]."

The federal judges therefore upheld what sovereignists have been saying for thirty years: after a Yes vote, there will be negotiations. At the time of the last referendum, we repeated this in all forums. Such was our conviction. Today it is a certainty, particularly considering that the representatives of the federal government admitted, yesterday, that they would act in accordance with the order that they themselves received from their Court.

In 1995, we played by the rules; we developed our negotiating position — the offer of partnership. We created an orientation and supervision committee for the negotiations. I even seem to recall that we appointed a chief negotiator.

The No side, for its part, wanted to raise fear among Quebecers. The next time, the men and women of Quebec will be able to vote Yes with the certainty that negotiations will take place and that everything will be set in motion for an orderly transition toward sovereignty, in the respect of the rights of each of our citizens, as we have always stated.

This element of good sense, I am profoundly convinced, now confers a considerable advantage upon the sovereignist project and constitutes one of the winning conditions of which I have been speaking for several years.

Third myth: the nature of the negotiations. Certain federalists have claimed that if negotiations ended up taking place after a Yes vote, they would deal not with sovereignty, but with a renewal of federalism.

Yesterday, the Court closed this avenue with a double lock. It stipulated, that "the negotiations [...] would address the potential act of secession as well as its possible terms should in fact secession proceed." The federal judges mentioned several elements that will have to be covered during these negotiations.

They recall, as we so often have, that Quebec and its neighbours share, "a national economy and a national debt." They also underline that the interests of Canada and of the provinces will have to be addressed in these negotiations. We have always said, and continue to think, that the economic interest of Canada, of the provinces, of the economy and of the debt must lead us to come to an agreement on a partnership that will preserve the common economic space between the two sovereign states.

The Court speaks of the necessary protection of the rights of minorities and states that it is necessary to take into account the interests of the aboriginal peoples. This is also our position, and this is why, in the *Act respecting the future of Quebec*, we made the following commitment: "The new constitution [of a sovereign Quebec] shall guarantee the English-speaking community that its identity and institutions will be preserved. It shall also recognize the right of the aboriginal nations to self-government on lands over which they have full ownership and their right to participate in the development of Quebec; in addition, the existing constitutional rights of the aboriginal nations shall be recognized in the constitution."

Quebec has always been at the forefront, within Canada, in recognizing the rights of aboriginal peoples, particularly since the resolution presented by René Lévesque in 1984 recognizing, for the first time in Canada, the existence of the aboriginal nations of Quebec.

In short, on the nature of the negotiations that will follow a Yes vote in a referendum, the Court imposes upon the federalist camp obligations that the sovereignists had long since assumed.

Fourth myth: according to the federalists, after a Yes vote, in the event of a deadlock in the negotiations, the citizens of Quebec would be prisoners within Canada; that they cannot get out.

I would like to say, first of all, that we have no doubt that after a Yes vote, the political and economic situation will oblige Quebec and Canada not only to negotiate, but also to quickly come to an agreement on sovereignty and on the conditions of economic partnership.

However, at least theoretically, the question must be asked of what would happen in the event of a deadlock in the negotiations. On this, the Supreme Court dares not provide a precise set of directions, but when it raises this eventuality, it in no event raises the hypothesis according to which Quebecers would have to resign themselves to remaining in Canada, and to renouncing their democratic decision. On the contrary, the Court raises only a single eventuality, namely that in which, in order to break the deadlock, Quebec alone would declare its sovereignty and call for international recognition.

Indeed, the Court writes that Quebec's behaviour and that of Canada during the negotiation will be, "evaluated [...] on the international plane." And the Court is categorical in adding, and again I quote, that "a Quebec that had negotiated in conformity with constitutional principles and values in the face of unreasonable intransigence on the part of other participants at the federal or provincial level would be more likely to be recognized [...]."

Moreover, the Court sets out in black and white, as we ourselves have stated since the deliberations of the Bélanger-Campeau Commission, "It is true that international law may well, depending on the circumstances, adapt to recognize a political and/or factual reality, regardless of the legality of the steps leading to its creation." Further, the Court again affirms, and again I quote, "It may be that a unilateral secession by Quebec would eventually be accorded legal status by Canada and other states [...]."

Hence, the sovereignists and the Bélanger-Campeau Commission state the truth: in the event of a deadlock in negotiations, "it is true" that international law may recognize Quebec's decision. Indeed, the Court sends a signal to the international community, indicating to it that after a Yes vote, if Canada and the provinces were to prove intransigent toward Quebec, then Quebec's recognition would thereby be facilitated. Thus the Court has just given us one of the supplementary conditions for the success of the negotiations.

The fifth and final federalist myth that was buried yesterday deals with the wording of the question and with the majority. Since the last referendum, a number of federalists have stated that the federal government should be involved in the drafting and in the approval of the question, or in the setting of a new threshold for the majority.

Yesterday, the Court in no way called into question the right of the National Assembly alone to decide on the wording of the question and on the threshold of the majority. The consensus within Quebec on this point is as clear as it is unshakable. Moreover, Plan B had the effect of consolidating the agreement between the political parties in Quebec on these points, as has been reiterated since yesterday by the leaders of the two opposition parties of the National Assembly.

The court limits itself to stating that the political authorities will make a political judgement on the clarity of the question. This is what elected officials do on a daily basis on all issues.

Our position on this is known: the 1995 question was so clear that 94% of Quebecers, a record of participation, went to the polls to vote on this capital issue; the question was so clear that the Prime Minister of Canada, in a speech to the nation, warned voters that the referendum vote meant "remaining or no longer being Canadian, staying in or leaving, that is the issue of the referendum."

Concerning the majority, the Court judges, as do we, that it must be clear. But it describes this clarity using the word "qualitative," rather than the word "quantitative." I quote the Court, when it writes "we refer to a 'clear' majority as a qualitative evaluation." Thus it does not call into question the quantity of votes required to declare a victory for the Yes side. The judges are familiar with the precedents in Canadian history, particularly that of Newfoundland, which entered Canada with a 52 per cent majority. Any juridical or political statement to the effect that a result of 50 per cent plus one was not sufficient would call into question the validity of the Newfoundland vote.

The reality is that the federalists learned yesterday from the Supreme Court that the clear, reasonable and logical process proposed to the citizens of Quebec by the sovereignists is legitimate and that they will have to negotiate its implementation after a winning referendum.

The Court thereby shakes the foundations of the federalist strategy, and undermines the arguments of fear and of the refusal to negotiate.

Taken by itself, the obligation placed on Canada to negotiate with Quebec dissipates the uncertainty that caused the refusal of the federalists to negotiate to weigh in the minds of many Quebecers. Today these Quebecers find reassurance: their Yes will force Canada to negotiate.

More and more of the men and women of Quebec will conclude that the time will soon come to decide, once and for all, to bring to an end our unsolvable quarrels with Canada, to build here the country of Quebec, and to negotiate, with our neighbours, a mutually beneficial relationship between equals.

Thank you.

6

A Letter from Stéphane Dion

Stéphane Dion

This letter from federal Intergovernmental Affairs Minister Stéphane Dion to Premier Lucien Bouchard was sent 26 August 1998.

Dear Mr. Premier:

During your press conference on August 21, you expressed satisfaction in the opinion of the Supreme Court concerning the legality of a unilateral secession. Please allow me to assure myself that your satisfaction is not selective.

The government of Canada has, of course, declared itself bound by all aspects of this ruling. You, on the other hand, only recognize its legal validity for others and not for you or your government.

You praise those passages that interest you and ignore the content — however obvious — of those passages that displease you. This game of light and shadows is damaging to your project, especially given that you need the greatest transparency to succeed in the highly uncertain adventure that negotiating secession in good faith would be.

It was precisely that obligation to negotiate that pleased you. The Court tells us that a clear majority in favour of secession in a referendum based on a clear question would be sufficiently legitimate to compel all parties involved to undertake negotiations on secession in good faith and in accordance with the principles of democracy, federalism, the rule of law and the protection of minorities.

In this obligation to negotiate, you see a "winning condition" for a possible third referendum. I see it as the confirmation of a legitimate right of our fellow citizens, a right well accepted in Canada and one I have consistently promoted since I entered politics. For example, I am quoted in *Le Soleil* of January 27, 1996, two days after my appointment as Minister, in the following terms: "If a strong majority of Quebecers unfortunately voted in favour of secession in response to a clear question, I believe that the rest of Canada has the moral obligation to negotiate the division of the territory."

There is, however, a point that cannot be ignored: given that this obligation to negotiate is reciprocal, it would also be binding on you, much more so than the negotiations you had in mind in case of a referendum victory in 1995. There are three fundamental differences.

1. Negotiations conditional on clear support for secession

You can no longer claim to be the sole judge of the clarity of the question and of the majority. The Court makes the obligation to negotiate conditional on obtaining a clear majority of Quebec electors responding in the affirmative to a clear question on secession. It leaves it to the political actors to judge the required clarity.

The National Assembly is of course free to ask Quebecers any questions it wants. But you will appreciate that the federal government, among others, cannot surrender its responsibility to evaluate the clarity of a question which could result in the break-up of the country.

A question that does not address secession, or that includes other topics, would not provide the assurance that Quebecers want to give up Canada. In order to trigger the obligation to negotiate, which you so enthusiastically welcome, there must be a clear response to a clear question on secession.

During your press conference you rejected the proposal put forward by Mr. Claude Ryan that would have given the Official Opposition in the National Assembly a right to examine the referendum question. But don't you believe that the opinion of the principal federalist party in Quebec would have an influence on the government of Canada's own evaluation of the clarity of the question?

The government of Canada could never undertake negotiations on secession based on a question addressing such vague concepts as "sovereignty-association" or "sovereignty with an offer of political and economic partnership." The risk of misinterpreting the vote would be too great, as many polls demonstrate.

Requiring that Quebecers be asked a clear question does not insult their intelligence. A clear question is an essential condition of a valid referendum in a democracy, in Quebec as elsewhere. Public consultations on attaining independence held in other parts of the world have almost always put a clear, simple question to voters.

As for the majority required to trigger negotiations on a secession, the Court tells us that its evaluation is qualitative in nature. There is no absolute legal standard on which to rely. You draw the conclusion that the Court invites us to be content with 50% + 1, a Quebec split in two. We do not share this interpretation because the quantity is relevant to evaluating the quality.

The Court, in its seventy-eight pages of advice, takes the trouble to link the negotiation of a secession no less than thirteen times to obtaining, beforehand, a "clear majority," three times to a "clear expression," twice to a "clear repudiation of the existing constitutional order," as well as once each to a "strong majority," to "results […] free of ambiguity" and to a "clear referendum result."

Many important decisions in society require qualified majorities. Thus, the Court mentions the need for a "substantial consensus" and "broad support in the form of an 'enhanced majority'" in order to effect important constitutional modifications. Furthermore, the Court states that secession would require a constitutional amendment and that these modifications would be "radical and extensive."

There are no examples of a successful secession based on a slender majority obtained through a referendum. When questioned on this point you were unable to refer to a single case during your press conference, and for good reason.

The government of Canada believes that a majority would need to be sufficiently clear to avoid any possibility of its collapsing under the pressure of the economic, social and other difficulties that an attempt at secession would undoubtedly cause. In addition, the size of the majority must be sufficient to legitimize such a radical change that would commit future generations. We must be wary of circumstantial majorities.

2. Negotiation of secession within the constitutional framework

You can no longer claim to effect a unilateral secession. Bill 1 on the Future of Quebec contemplated a one-year period of negotiation on a political and economic partnership, "unless the National Assembly decides otherwise." The National Assembly could unilaterally declare the independence of Quebec at any point. This declaration would have been perfectly legal, according to your own erroneous interpretation of international law.

After reading the opinion of the Supreme Court, no one can not know that such an attempt at unilateral secession would have had no legal basis. International law gives you no right to effect independence unilaterally while ignoring the Canadian legal order. At no point in the process would the law authorize you to take it upon yourself to deprive us, Quebecers, of our full belonging in Canada.

The Court does not rule out the possibility of your attempting a unilateral secession, but the scenario it describes bears little resemblance to the one you contemplated in 1995. The Court says that such an attempt would be without "colour of a legal right" and in a context in which Canada is entitled "to the protection under international law of its territorial integrity." The Court simply says that the chances of international recognition would be better if the government of Quebec negotiated in good faith while its counterparts showed unreasonable intransigence. Even under such a highly implausible scenario, we can question whether the international community would overcome its well-known aversion to unilateral secessions.

A unilateral secession would be impracticable. If, regardless of the law, you decided to proclaim yourself the government of an independent state, citizens and governments would be within their rights not to consider you as such and to continue to act peacefully within the Canadian legal order. You cannot by an act contrary to law take Canada away from millions of Quebecers who would consider themselves to still be Canadians.

Any future negotiations on secession would have to take place within the Canadian constitutional framework, not between two independent states. Secession would be proclaimed only after a separation agreement accompanied by a constitutional amendment.

3. Negotiations of secession whose content cannot be predicted

You can no longer claim that you alone would determine what would be on the negotiating table. The Court does not recognize a right to secession, it establishes only the right to negotiate in good faith.

The Court explains that these negotiations would relate to much more than just the "negotiation of the logistical details of secession": "There would be no conclusions predetermined by law on any issue. Negotiations would need to address the interests of the other provinces, the federal government, Quebec and indeed the rights of all Canadians both within and outside Quebec, and specifically the rights of minorities."

The Court also recognizes "the importance of the submissions made to us respecting the rights and concerns of aboriginal peoples in the event of a unilateral secession, as well as the appropriate means of defining the boundaries of a seceding Quebec with particular regard to the northern lands occupied largely by aboriginal peoples."

Addressing the legitimate interests called into question by secession will raise the issue of the boundaries of Quebec. "Arguments were raised before us regarding boundary issues. [...] Nobody seriously suggests that our national existence, seamless in so many aspects, could be effortlessly separated along what are now the provincial boundaries of Quebec."

The Court warns of the difficulty of the negotiations: "No one can predict the course that such negotiations might take." This is the beginning of the black hole that the leader of the Quebec Liberal Party, Jean Charest, has always rightly warned us of.

In short, the obligation to negotiate secession, which the Supreme Court has just given a constitutional dimension, itself depends on clear support for secession, respect for the constitutional framework and a great deal of mutual good faith. If your government fails to observe these principles of clarity, legality and good faith, the constitutional obligation to negotiate no longer holds.

Negotiations on secession based on the clear support of Quebecers, conducted legally, and with a concern for justice for all: this is the only way to achieve independence for Quebec. The time for stratagems and "winning" tricks is over.

Instead of concocting the question that will snatch a few thousand more votes, do your job. Explain to us Quebecers why we would be happier if we were no longer Canadians as well; why we need a smaller country that is ours alone, rather than a larger country shared with others. If you convince us, the question and the majority will follow. The referendum will then merely confirm a visible consensus. Firmly determined to separate, Quebecers could wade through the problems of the negotiations.

If this is a tall order, it is certainly not the fault of the federal government. It is simply that it must be very hard to give up Canada, a country that you yourself described in 1988 as "a land of promise [...] celebrated for its generosity and tolerance." Quebecers have contributed tremendously to building Canada and it is in working with other Canadians that they want to take on the enormous challenges presented at the dawn of the new millennium. It is up to you to prove to them, in all clarity, that they are wrong.

Sincerely,
Stéphane Dion

A Most Politic Judgement

Robert A. Young

Robert Young teaches at the Department of Political Science, University of Western Ontario. This essay is abridged from the original version which appeared in Constitutional Forum constitutionnel *10 (1998): 14-18.*

Introduction

By throwing before the Supreme Court a set of questions about Quebec secession, the Minister of Justice of Canada and his government could have profoundly disturbed the Canadian political system. In posing and answering questions about Quebecers' right to attain sovereignty and the modalities of achieving Quebec secession, the Minister and the Court risked igniting in Quebec a nationalist firestorm that could have sent support for sovereignty soaring. But the justices of the Court avoided this eventuality. They produced a compact judgement, one that has three important consequences. First and foremost, the Court managed to preserve its own legitimacy, despite having been dragged onto a hotly contested political terrain. Second, while positing an exhaustive constitution and claiming unparalleled scope for judges to interpret it, the Court managed to preserve a great deal of political space; that is, an area in which contending arguments about Quebec secession can be debated, with the political process determining the outcomes. Third, while explicitly preserving this political space, the Court also managed to narrow it constructively, by eliminating two radical positions about secession from the set of arguments about Quebec sovereignty that are decent, respectable and legitimate.

Legitimacy

Both when the Reference case was launched and when it was heard, sovereignist and nationalist politicians in Quebec attacked the federal government's move. Justice Minister Rock's tone in the House of Commons was moderate; more significantly, by asking the Court to address the issue of how Quebec secession *should* occur, the federal government admitted clearly for the first time that it *could* occur. Nevertheless, the sovereignists decried the federal strategy as one of intimidation and oppression, and one that should be rejected outright. As Mr. Bouchard argued, "there is only one tribunal to settle Quebec's political future and that's the Quebec people."[1] Even moderate Quebec nationalists and those politicians like Mr. Johnson and Mr. Charest who would have to appeal to them in elections declared that the Reference was ill-advised. It was preferable to move forward on the Plan A side (accommodating Quebecers' legitimate desire for change) rather than the Plan B front (clarifying the process of secession and making its costs more obvious to the electorate).

In ROC (the rest of Canada), there was no publicly discernible counterpart to this barrage on the Court, though a decision favourable to some aspects of the sovereignist position — such as that the required majority was 50% + 1 — could have produced one. The real danger was in Quebec, where the hard-line sovereignists insisted that the Court's purview did not extend to the political decisions taken by *le peuple québécois*. And this is the threat that was removed by the Court's logical dexterity.

What is the structure of the judgement, after all? There is a brief introduction (paras. 1–3) and a discussion of whether the three questions posed are justiciable (paras. 4–31). Then follows the bulk of the judgement, built around Question 1 (paras. 32–108). Here, the Court discusses Canadian history (paras. 32–48) and some of the constitutional principles that are relevant to the reference (paras. 49–82) before moving to the core of the judgement, "The Operation of the Constitutional Principles in the Secession Context" (paras. 83–105). A brief discussion of effectivity (paras. 106–8) — the assertion that effective political control over a given territory is sufficient to establish a new state under international law — concludes the section. Question 2 is treated at much less length (paras. 109–46, just about half the length of Question 1), and Question 3 is dispensed with in a single paragraph. A summary follows (paras. 148–56). So, almost one-half of the 116 substantive paragraphs is devoted to laying the historical and constitutional foundation for the core section.

Here is where the Court saved its own bacon. It argued that four constitutional principles were relevant in the reference: federalism, democracy, constitutionalism and the rule of law, and the protection of minorities. It rolled out a barrage of precedents to show how the Constitution is infused with these principles (and how courts have the power and the duty to define them). And it declared at the outset that "these defining principles function in symbiosis. *No single principle can be defined in isolation from the others, nor does any one principle trump or exclude the operation of any other*" (para. 49, emphasis added). It was this dictate that allowed the "Secession Context" section to deliver something to each side in the political contest over secession. The federalists got the judgement that secession must occur according to the rule of law, constitutionally, and with regard for the interests of all Canadians and of minorities within Quebec. The Court ruled that a unilateral secession — through a unilateral declaration of independence (UDI) — does not meet this standard. The sovereignists in turn got satisfaction from the Court's treatment of the democratic principle in a secession. A Yes vote would carry weight, the Court said, "in that it would confer legitimacy on the efforts of the government of Quebec to initiate the Constitution's amendment process in order to secede by constitutional means" (para. 87). Such a vote "would give rise to a reciprocal obligation on all parties to Confederation to negotiate constitutional changes to respond to that desire," because "the corollary of a legitimate attempt by one participant in Confederation to seek an amendment to the Constitution is an obligation on all parties to come to the negotiating table" (para. 88).

After a very brief period of hesitation, the sovereignists declared victory. Mr. Brassard, then Quebec Minister for Intergovernmental Affairs, claimed that the Court had "recognized the democratic legitimacy of both the option and the process leading up to the realization of the sovereignty project." Mr. Parizeau said that the threat of a UDI had been necessary in the past to get ROC to the bargaining table after a Yes vote; now, however, the justices "say that the two sides have an obligation to negotiate in good faith. We say fine."[2] The next day, Mr. Bouchard called a news conference. He claimed that the judgement had destroyed five "federalist myths" and more generally that the Court "affirmed, from one end of its opinion to the other, the political nature of the process that would legitimately be set in motion by a Quebec referendum on sovereignty." In particular, the "federal judges upheld what sovereignists have been saying for thirty years: after a Yes vote, there will be negotiations."[3] The Premier had nothing critical to say about the judgement; instead he used it to shore up the sovereignist interpretation of the process of secession.

All in all, the sovereignists accepted the judgement. Of course they dismissed or downplayed those aspects of it that comforted the federalists — the need for a clear question, a clear majority and a lawful process. But they used the Court to substantiate their own position. In fact, one former Bloc MP predicted that "no one should be surprised to see the Supreme Court of Canada quoted in future campaign literature and on the posters of the Parti Québécois." The judgement, in a sense, came to underpin and reinforce their arguments about secession. So rather than losing legitimacy, the Court found its political position substantially strengthened in Quebec. No doubt the sovereignists were prepared for a full-scale attack on the Court and were ready to undermine its authority; indeed, some tried to do this in the wake of the judgement. But this extreme position found no backers in the party leadership (or among most editorialists). Instead, by using the judgement toward their own ends, the sovereignists strengthened the Court.

This is terribly important. Were there to be a Yes vote in the future, or even a referendum, the Court might be brought in to rule on highly contentious matters. The justices were undoubtedly aware of this possibility. Even as they tossed back into the political arena important issues like the clarity of the question and the required magnitude of a referendum vote for sovereignty, and circumscribed their own current role (paras. 98–105), they hinted at decisions that might come: "in accordance with the usual rule of prudence in constitutional cases, we refrain from pronouncing on the applicability of any particular constitutional procedure to effect secession unless and until sufficiently clear facts exist to squarely raise an issue for judicial determination" (para. 105). In the course of an attempted secession, the Court might be the only body able to decide procedural matters such as who participates in negotiations and how the Constitution must be amended in order to effect secession, as well as substantive matters such as minority rights and citizenship. Because of its great prudence in the Reference case, and the subtle balance it struck, the Court will take into any future secession a large enough stock of legitimacy to make authoritative decisions. This is the greatest success of the judgement.

Political Space

Having defined the constitutional principles relevant to secession, the Court preserved a large political arena for debate. It left open some very important questions:

- The amending formula necessary to effect secession
- What constitutes a "clear majority"
- What constitutes a "clear question"
- What would be the content of negotiations after a Yes vote
- What parties would be involved in the negotiations
- What are the rights of linguistic and cultural minorities, including aboriginals
- What would happen in the case of an impasse in negotiations

Not surprisingly, intense political debate began immediately around these issues as well as the ambiguities in the judgement itself. Stéphane Dion was especially quick to reply to Mr. Bouchard's interpretation of the Court's position. This was perfectly appropriate, in the view of the justices, as they had merely defined the broad constitutional framework within which such debate would occur, both before and after any future referendum on secession. "Having established the legal framework," they wrote, "it would be for the democratically elected leadership of the various participants to resolve their differences" (para. 101). The Court spent some time justifying the maintenance of this political space (paras. 98–102) on the grounds of precedent and practicality, and this restraint along with the Court's evenhandedness undoubtedly helped preserve its legitimacy.

Nevertheless, the justices did make one powerful foray to constrain the realm of political debate. In a manoeuvre that lies right at the heart of the judgement (paras. 90–93), they eliminated extremists from the legitimate political arena. Here, the Court rejected two "absolutist propositions" (para. 90). Against radical sovereignists, it held that "Quebec could not purport to invoke a right of self-determination such as to dictate the terms of a proposed secession to other parties" (para. 91). In other words, the principle of democracy cannot override the obligation to respect the other three principles and to negotiate within the broad constitutional framework. This would strip the legitimacy from a hard-nosed Quebec bargaining posture backed up by the threat of a UDI. At the other extreme, the Court rejected the view that a clear Yes vote could be ignored, because "this would amount to the assertion that other constitutional principles necessarily trump the clearly expressed democratic will of the people of Quebec" (para. 92). This undercuts the 10 or 15% of citizens in ROC who would prefer to ignore or repress a move by Quebecers towards sovereignty. Taken together, these central paragraphs constitute a ringing blow for moderation. While the justices left a great deal of room for political argument, they tossed the extremists out of court, and tilted the political playing field on both sides toward moderation and civility rather than polarization.

8

How to Deny Quebec's Right to Self-Determination

Josée Legault

This article by Josée Legault was carried on 21 August 1998 in The Globe and Mail. *She is a political scientist, author, and columnist for* The Gazette *in Montreal.*

The historic opinion handed down yesterday by the Supreme Court of Canada is a veritable imposture. Hiding behind its alleged "judicial" nature, it is in fact a direct political assault on Quebec's right to fully and freely decide its own future.

Once again, and with the full force of their unelected and unanswerable posts, these nine judges, these nine creatures of the federal executive power, have proved that they are political mercenaries working to reinforce the Canadian state, that they are tools used by Ottawa to combat Quebec's affirmation. In Quebec, it is high time we denounced them for what they are. In Canada, the "rule of law," the Constitution and the higher courts have become strong and willing obstacles in the way of Quebec's eventual accession to independence.

Let us first recall the political objectives of the federal government when it demanded this opinion in 1996: (1) to deny the existence of a Quebec nation by submitting to the Supreme Court justices its very right to self-determination; (2) to destabilize undecided voters by imposing the beginnings of a highly complex set of rules; (3) to favour the partition movement in Quebec by creating the illusion that a majority Yes vote would not be decisive as long as we did not get approval from the rest of Canada (ROC); (4) to endanger the international recognition of a sovereign Quebec by transforming that recognition into a gesture of defiance toward Canadian law.

Each of these objectives was met in yesterday's decision. Guy Bertrand's radiant white smile of joy and ultimate satisfaction, over all the television networks, confirmed it without a doubt.

With this court opinion, we have left what Robert Bourassa used to denounce as "dominating federalism" and entered the realm of a more colonialist type of federalism, a contradiction in terms if ever there were one. This colonialist federalism is at the heart of the Court's opinion — a court named by the Prime Minister of Canada, responsible for the interpretation of a Constitution that has not been ratified by Quebec and was written with the clear intention to reduce Quebec's powers.

This Court's opinion clearly confirms the rupture we experienced in this country in the last referendum. It is imbued with the kind of provocative colonial vision that has shown itself since October 1995, through the so-called Plan B and partitionist movements. After having denied our traditional right of veto in 1981, after having facilitated the 1982 patriation without Quebec's consent, after having destroyed sections of our Charter of the French Language, after having gutted our referendum law, the Supreme Court has now added a new weapon against Quebec by submitting its right of self-determination to the veto of Ottawa and English Canada. This is not the rule of law; this is the rule of the mightiest.

The Court's opinion subjugates Quebec by insisting that it would be up to the "clear majority" before the next referendum. While the Parti Québécois has always said that any partnership or association would, quite logically, be negotiated with the ROC, the Court's opinion takes away the National Assembly's right to define the question and denies the universally accepted majority rule of 50 per cent plus one.

The political actors the Court refers to are most probably Ottawa, the ROC, the linguistic minorities and the aboriginals. Thus, Quebec loses its right of self-determination when the Court dictates that the rules preceding the next referendum should be set by the entire country. This is appalling and unacceptable.

Thus, it is no longer the partnership that would be negotiable, but the democratic process leading to the referendum and sovereignty itself. This is a flagrant denial of Quebec as a nation, free to determine its own future. To submit the "rules" to Ottawa and the ROC for approval is like asking David to negotiate the rules of combat with Goliath.

With this decision, the authority of the State of Quebec and its nation is under attack. The Bouchard government can only reply with the voice of the election. We can no longer just speak; we must act. The government must resist the temptation not to act. This Court's opinion is not in any way of a judicial nature. It is purely political. Therefore, it must be countered by political means.

One cannot simply ignore the possible effects of the Court's decision on the eventual international recognition of a sovereign Quebec and on undecided voters. Time is running out for Quebec. Within the next 15 years francophones stand to become a minority on the island of Montreal, and the federal state, along with its Supreme Court ally, will continue trying to keep Quebec from becoming independent.

Sovereignists must therefore quickly rebuild and strengthen their rainbow coalition of 1995. To counter the effects of the Court's decision on the international scene, Quebec must also rebuild its network of foreign delegations and staff them with the most competent analysts and communicators. It remains incomprehensible why the sovereignty movement does not give itself comparable means to defend its option to those of the federalists.

To mobilize and sensitize the situation Quebec population to the gravity of the situation, the PQ must promote its option seven days a week. In a democracy, one must convince in order to win. This was almost achieved in 1995. Let us make sure the next time is the right one.

However many experts may marvel at the alleged nuances of the Court's decision, its message is clear: The federal government, through its Supreme Court, is taking away our right to decide our future. In Quebec, the time has come for great solidarity, willpower and lucidity. The realm of politics must reclaim its power from non-elected judges whose work aims to weaken Quebec.

Let us take the means that will ensure that Quebecers will hold their next referendum freely. Without this freedom, there can be no referendum. Without a referendum, there can be no independence. That is exactly what the Court and Ottawa understand. That is why we are now faced with this attempt to deny us our right to self-determination. To protect our future in Quebec, we must not let them succeed.

9

The Supreme Court Ruling: A Legitimate and Achievable Secession ... in Theory

Jacques-Yvan Morin
Translated by Eric Hamovitch

This article by Jacques-Yvan Morin, Professor Emeritus of Public Law at the University of Montreal, was published in Le Devoir *on 31 August 1998.*

The Supreme Court's answers to the questions put by the federal government on the subject of Quebec secession while not lacking in juridical finesse, do abound in political trickery. On the one hand, secession is possible and legitimate in theory. Ottawa and English Canada cannot take "the right to pursue secession" away from Quebec. On the other hand, however, the Supreme Court ruling knowingly or inadvertently gives the federal authorities the right to erect such substantial and numerous hurdles that this obstacle course will require Quebecers to show enormous will, cohesion, and political dexterity.

Early in their reasoning, the judges were able to rise to a plane that might have been expected of them by the legal world, especially at the international level — the group of jurists and diplomats who are increasingly well informed about the Canadian crisis and curious about the attitudes of a state that always seems inclined to preach virtue to others.

Later, however, the Court could not avoid again becoming the federal organ it has always been in constitutional matters. It gives the federal authorities more tools than required to obstruct the Quebec referendum process and, if the Yes side were to win, to derail the subsequent negotiations and provoke the abortion of any constitutional revision leaning toward sovereignty for the Quebec state.

Leaning on basic principles that underlie the federal constitution — democracy, federalism, rule of law and respect for minorities — the Court pulls out two imperatives that have been kept silent, if not obliterated, since the 1995 referendum: respect on Canada's part for a sovereignty project supported democratically by a majority of Quebecers, and an obligation for the "two majorities" to negotiate the conditions of secession. By this yardstick, the behaviour of a number of federal politicians has been unconstitutional for quite some time.

It is not a matter of indifference to know that the existing Constitution gives the sovereignist project just as sure a legitimacy as the various proposals for institutional transformation that have been made over the last few years — just as legitimate, in any case, as the repatriation and the amending formula imposed unilaterally upon Quebec by English Canada and Mr. Trudeau in 1982.

For the Court, a will to "effect secession" even constitutes "a right" of the Quebec government, provided the means of seeking this result are democratic and orderly.

This finally puts to rest the opinion heard now and again — unfortunately from the mouths of more than one English Canadian jurist — suggesting that any attempt to promote sovereignty constitutes treason. It will be awkward for some of them to call for the bombing of Quebec's hydroelectric dams by the Canadian air force in the event of secession! And the federal authorities, unless they are totally lacking in judgement, will have to give up on threats of reprisals or other Plan B schemes.

The theme of negotiations between Canada and Quebec reappears as a *leitmotif* in the Court's ruling. The "obligation" to negotiate is made necessary by the freely expressed will to move on to sovereignty. We may observe in passing that this obligation already exists according to the current Constitution, but has not produced any tangible result in the nearly forty years that the Quebec–Canada conflict has lasted. Despite remonstrances from Quebec, the government in Ottawa preferred to act unilaterally both when it ended judicial appeals to the British Privy Council (which had protected Quebec's autonomy) and when it "repatriated" the Constitution. This intransigence was a major cause of the alienation of the Quebec people. A lot of good it does for the Court to urge negotiations *in extremis*.

That answers, in theory, the refusal to negotiate and the threats issued by federal politicians. Will it suffice to put an end to threats of intimidation before and after the vote? The early federal reactions seem to indicate the contrary.

For its part, the Quebec government has always known and said it would negotiate, even showing some elements of compromise such as economic union and the free movement of people and goods. Only the firm refusal to negotiate displayed by the federal authorities caused Premier Jacques Parizeau to raise the possibility of a unilateral declaration at the expiration of a fixed interval.

What would happen in case of refusal or of blockage in the negotiations, a hypothesis that seems more than plausible? The Court is conscious of this possibility and avoids the issue, saying that it does not have to conjecture as to what would happen then. It recognizes, however, the possibility of an unconstitutional declaration ending in *de facto* secession. It adds that, certainly, this power would be exercised without a juridical basis, but it feels the ultimate success of secession would then depend on the recognition of the existence of the new sovereign state by the international community, which would presumably take into consideration the conduct of both Quebec and Canada.

The Court goes even further: envisaging the case of a people prevented from usefully exercising its right to self-determination within the state it is part of, it writes that so complete an obstruction could give birth to the right to secession, referring to the doctrine of international law. Although it does not wish to decide whether this forms a firmly established standard, it can be seen as a subtle warning to the federal government: an unconstitutional secession can succeed at the international level; it is thus better to negotiate.

Similarly, a Quebec that negotiated in good faith but in vain would "be more likely to be recognized."

The judges have thus defined certain standards of behaviour in a way that cannot be harmful to Quebec, taking account of its continuous willingness to negotiate. By doing this the Court has even, *obiter dictum*, thrown away the federal right of disallowance, which had fallen into disuse but could have been part of the Plan B arsenal. Moreover, this first aspect of its work, of an essentially juridical character, was carried out with a pedagogical touch that we should be grateful for.

Unfortunately, the questions left open by the Court are numerous and constitute an array of blunt instruments left within reach of the federal authorities.

10

Liberal Party Wins, Canada Loses

Ted Morton

This article by Ted Morton appeared in the Ottawa Citizen *on 22 August 1998. Ted Morton teaches political science at the University of Calgary.*

There are only two relevant questions to be asked about the Supreme Court ruling on the legality of a unilateral declaration of independence (UDI) by Quebec. First, has the Liberal government's Plan B strategy of using the Reference brought the nation any closer to defeating the separatists and bringing closure to this financially ruinous episode of Canadian history? Second, what did the Supreme Court contribute to this result, or non-result, as the case may be?

The answer to the first question is a resounding NO! Despite all the frenzied constitutional chatter that the national media has once again dumped on the beleaguered Canadian public, we are not one step closer to closure on the Quebec neverendum. Indeed, despite the English media's slavish and mentally lazy recycling of Liberal spin-artists' claims that the Court has "clarified" the issue of UDI, the Court's ruling has actually complicated the matter by arming the separatists with new legal rights.

Contrary to early media reports, the Court's ruling was not simply a "win" for Ottawa. Yes, the Court ruled that UDI was illegal under both Canadian domestic and international law. But this hardly qualifies as news.

At least outside of Quebec, there has never been any question that the separation of Quebec from Canada would be a major change in the Canadian Constitution and require a formal amendment — and thus the consent of the other provinces — to be legal.

To dispel any doubt about this, imagine a "UEQ" — a unilateral expulsion of Quebec from Confederation by the nine other provinces and Ottawa via a successful referendum. Would the Supreme Court uphold the legality of a UEQ? Clearly not. And yet Quebec would have us believe that what would be illegal for nine other provinces acting together would be legal for one province acting alone? Please!

As for international law, the second question addressed by the Court, success confers its own legitimacy. UDI is a revolutionary act. When revolutions succeed, the leaders become presidents and prime ministers. When revolutions fail, the leaders are shot for treason, at least in the rest of the civilized world. The Court argued earnestly that UDI was also illegal under international law. But in the end, it was forced to concede the obvious: "secession of a province from Canada, if successful in the streets, might well lead to the creation of a new state." As Jean Charest said over a year ago, this Reference could not tell us anything that we didn't already know.

The real "news" in this ruling is the asterisk beside "win*"; the judicial "but on the other hand" statements. In a feeble attempt at what passes these days for statesmanship, the Court was determined to give something to both sides. And give they did.

Buried deep in the middle of the judgement (para. 92), is the following startling statement: "The rights of other provinces and the federal government cannot deny the right of the government of Quebec to pursue secession, should a clear majority of the people of Quebec choose that goal."

Here, for the first time ever, the Supreme Court has created (it certainly can't be found anywhere in the text of the Constitution) a constitutional "right to pursue secession." And of course, where there are rights, there are corollary duties. And so the Court goes on to tell us that if the separatists were to win a referendum "by a clear majority on a clear question," then Canada has a "constitutional duty to negotiate." Indeed, the Court goes on to say that there is corollary obligation to negotiate in "good faith."

So there you have the real news. As of August 1998, Quebec now has, in writing, a "constitutional right" to pursue secession and Canada has a "constitutional duty to negotiate." Translated into ordinary English, then, here is the message that the Court has sent to Quebec: "UDI is illegal, unless you can get away with it. And if you win a fairly worded referendum, Ottawa has a constitutional duty to negotiate with you in good faith. Indeed, if Ottawa doesn't negotiate in good faith, then you are justified in getting away with it."

Not bad for second place!

While the Supreme Court richly deserves to be criticized for making such unnecessary concessions to the separatists, it is hardly the most guilty party. The Court was caught up in the dilemma created by the Liberals' own "lose/lose" strategy. A complete legal victory could provoke a backlash — and thus a political loss — in Quebec. But conceding something to Quebec would be to give the separatists more than they had before.

Predictably but wrongly, the Supreme Court chose the latter as the lesser evil. Predictable, because we can hardly expect the cabinet-appointed judges to show more backbone than those who have appointed them. Wrong, because prior to yesterday's ruling, a Quebec UDI had no legitimacy outside of Quebec. It was illegal. Period. Yesterday's ruling changed this. As one Southam editorialist has written: "Canada cannot deal summarily with Quebec separatism. It is required by law to negotiate." If this is what winning means, I would hate to see a loss!

The Supreme Court should never have agreed to hear the UDI Reference in the first place. It was clear that the Liberal government was using the Court for purely political purposes. Its protests to the contrary notwithstanding, the Court has unfettered discretion to refuse to answer Reference questions that it views as too abstract or too political. The Court has done so in the past. Why didn't it refuse this time?

The answer is part judicial ego and part political. For the justices to refuse to hear the UDI Reference would have denied themselves the political limelight to which they have become so accustomed. Here was the Court's opportunity to dance on the political centre-stage in a case our ever modest Chief Justice had described (with his usual gift of understatement) as "the most important case ever heard by the Supreme Court."

More importantly, the Court is politically on side on the national unity issue. Here, the Quebec nationalist take is much clearer than the view propagated in English Canada. Contrary to the theory that the Court acts as a "check" on the national government, on this (and certain other issues) the Supreme Court is more an ally. Like the Trudeau, Mulroney and Chrétien governments who appointed them, the judges subscribe to Ottawa's official credo of "unity at any price." For the national political class, of which the Supreme Court justices are all central members, no price is too high to avoid the unthinkable. Helping out the Liberals on the UDI Reference was easy.

The Liberals' UDI Reference was an attempt to do indirectly through the Court what Chrétien and his Quebec ministers don't have the courage to do directly: to lay down clear ground rules for any Quebec separation; to spell out in advance of any future referendum a specific process and Canada's minimum conditions for a negotiated secession.

This is the step required to signal to Quebec voters the true price of separation and to reduce the political uncertainty associated with separatist referenda. It is this uncertainty that is driving the market crazy and the dollar down. Enacting such contingency legislation is the approach that has been advocated by parties as diverse as the C.D. Howe Institute and the Reform Party. But the Chrétien Liberals don't have the courage to do so. Not surprisingly, the Supreme Court didn't either.

In sum, after two years (really, two decades), millions of dollars of legal fees, court costs, consultants' bills, pools of news ink, reels of video tape, shelves of books and articles — yes, after "the most important decision ever made by the Supreme Court" — we are not one step closer to closure on this financially ruinous era of Canadian history.

Any impartial observer would have to judge this to be bad for Canada. A colossal waste of time and money. But what the mainstream media refuse to point out is that this sorry state of affairs is actually good news for the Liberal Party. It gives Mr. Chrétien the appearance of having done something (when in fact he hasn't) and buys more time.

And that's all the Liberals need — the illusion of action and time. It's not in the Liberals' interest to "solve" the national unity crisis. Far better just "manage" it. As long as there is a "national unity crisis," Canadians will be taught to believe that we "need" the Liberals to broker it. God forbid that some other party be given such a sacred trust!

The "national unity" issue is the Liberals' ticket to staying in power. On Thursday, the Supreme Court graciously punched it. And so, the neverendum marches on. This is good news for the Liberals but bad news for Canada.

11

The Quebec Secession Reference: Some Unexpected Consequences of Constitutional First Principles

José Woehrling

This article originally appeared in Canada Watch *in February 1999 (Vol. 7, no. 1). José Woehrling teaches law at the University of Montreal.*

Not surprisingly, in the Quebec Secession Reference, the federal government has obtained some of the answers it obviously hoped for in referring its questions to the Supreme Court.

Thus, the Court states that secession of a province could not be achieved unilaterally under the Constitution of Canada ("unilaterally" being defined by the Court as meaning "without principled negotiation with other participants in Confederation within the existing constitutional framework"). Regarding the right to self-determination that belongs to peoples under international law, the Court rules that a right to secession only arises where a people is subject to alien subjugation, domination or exploitation; and possibly where a people is denied its right to self-determination within the state of which it forms a part. Assuming that the Quebec population forms a "people," Quebec does not meet any of the requirements necessary for the right to secession. However, although there is no right to unilateral secession under the Constitution or at international law, the possibility of an unconstitutional declaration of secession leading to a *de facto* secession is not ruled out. The ultimate success of such a secession would be dependent on recognition by the international community, which is likely to consider the legality and legitimacy of secession having regard to, amongst other facts, the conduct of Quebec and Canada.

Thus, it has now been clearly established by the Court that a unilateral declaration of independence (UDI), such as contemplated in the bill introduced by the Parizeau government before the 1995 referendum and referred to in the referendum question, would be unconstitutional. Should another separatist government embark on the same strategy, the Supreme Court ruling will make it easier for the federal government, or indeed any citizen, to challenge its validity or even to ask for a court order prohibiting a new referendum.

However, the Court's decision also contains a number of elements that were assuredly not desired by the federal government and will almost inevitably assist the cause of the Quebec sovereignists.

First, the Court proclaims the "democratic legitimacy" of a secession initiative approved by a clear majority vote in Quebec on a clear question. In the past, certain commentators in the rest of Canada have affirmed that the mere attempt to separate Quebec from Canada was illegitimate and even illegal. Such arguments have now been put to rest. It is true that the highest federal authorities have sometimes recognized that it would be difficult, on a political level, to refuse any negotiations with Quebec after a positive referendum on secession. Yet the Court goes much further by stating that, in such a case, the rest of Canada would have a constitutional and legal obligation to negotiate. This is very important, because politicians in the other provinces have occasionally proclaimed that they would altogether refuse to negotiate with a secessionist Quebec. Now that it is clear that a victorious referendum will trigger negotiations, a certain number of "soft nationalists" in Quebec will be less hesitant to vote Yes in the future. Some of them will probably act in this way in the hope that at some point in the negotiations the object will shift and become a renewal of federalism instead of secession.

The second favourable element for the sovereignists is that the Court seems to give little importance to the constitutional amending formula in the event of a secession. During the hearings of the Reference before the Supreme Court, counsel for the federal government put considerable weight on the argument that the secession of a province can only be conducted through the amending formula. This would mean that Quebec has to obtain the separate approval of the legislative assemblies of the nine other provinces as well as of both houses of Parliament (the Court says nothing about the applicable amending formula, but for the great majority of constitutional lawyers, secession would require the unanimity procedure). In addition, if the Charlottetown referendum is to be considered as a political precedent, Quebec's accession to independence would also have to be approved in a popular referendum by a majority of all Canadian voters as well as by a majority in each of the five "regions." By insisting on compliance with such a cumbersome procedure, the federal government was able to claim that it abstractly recognized the right of Quebecers to decide their own constitutional future while at the same time denying such a right on a practical and political level.

The Court brings this scheme to ruin by establishing a sequence of events that leaves only a secondary role for the amending formula. Should Quebecers approve secession, negotiations would be held on the precise conditions. If the negotiations failed, there would be of course no need to use the amending formula (but the Court acknowledges that a failure attributable to bad faith on the part of the rest of Canada could facilitate a Quebec UDI). If, on the other hand, negotiations succeeded, recourse to the amending formula would still be required, but it is difficult to see how a province or the federal government could then refuse its formal approval, and thus negate the political agreement arrived at. However, should this happen, the Court recognizes that Quebec could then try the UDI route and that such a course would be subject to evaluation by the international community, each foreign state having to take a position based on its judgement of the conduct during negotiations of Quebec and the rest of Canada, respectively (para. 103).

In other words — and this is a third favourable element for the sovereignists — the Supreme Court recognizes the linkage that exists between constitutional and international law as to the possibility of a secession. If the Quebec sovereignists take unreasonable positions in the negotiations and then issue a UDI, other states will hesitate to recognize it. On the contrary, if it is the rest of Canada that negotiates in bad faith, or proves incapable of ratifying a negotiated settlement because of the difficulties of the amending formula, the international community may be inclined to grant recognition to a Quebec UDI. Thus, the reaction of other states to the conduct of Quebec and

Canada underpins the obligation to negotiate that both Quebec and Canada are under.

It must be stressed that an attempt to secede is the only kind of constitutional modification where a judgement by the international community gives force to the obligation to negotiate that the Court declares to exist in the case of any initiative for constitutional amendment. The reason for this is that secession inevitably has consequences on an international and diplomatic plane. The same is obviously not true of other amendment initiatives, for example, Senate reform. Should the Western provinces hold a successful referendum on the Triple E Senate and launch a formal amendment initiative, the rest of Canada would be under an obligation to negotiate, but the failure of the negotiation and the respective conduct of the parties to it would remain a strictly Canadian matter and be of no interest to the international community (unless the rejection of their demands leads the Western provinces to attempt secession from Canada).

Finally, and this fourth element is already contained in the preceding one, the Court makes it clear that any negotiations on secession must be conducted bilaterally, between Quebec and the rest of Canada, and not multilaterally, between Quebec, on the one side, and each province and the federal government, on the other side:

> The negotiation process precipitated by a decision of a clear majority of the population of Quebec on a clear question to pursue secession would require the reconciliation of various rights and obligations by the representatives of two legitimate majorities, namely, the clear majority of the population of Quebec, and the clear majority of Canada as a whole, whatever that may be (para. 93).

The Court, so to speak, enjoins Canada to speak with one voice during the negotiations with Quebec. This is crucial because one way of indirectly refusing to negotiate secession, present in the writings of some ROC academics, is to claim that the rest of Canada could not possibly agree on a common position vis-à-vis Quebec, any attempted negotiations being thus doomed to fail.

In the text of the Reference, the Court stresses many times that the obligation of the rest of Canada to negotiate will only be triggered by "a clear majority vote in Quebec on a clear question in favour of secession." However, the Court leaves it to the political actors to determine what these notions mean. I have already taken a position on these subjects.[1] The question in a future referendum should be agreed to by all political parties present in the Quebec Legislative Assembly. In a situation where the Parti Québécois formed the government, the Official Opposition would be the Liberal Party of Quebec, a political party strongly opposed to secession. Nobody could thus claim that the question was unclear or ambiguous. Such a solution avoids the inextricable problems that would exist if the federal government demanded to participate in the formulation of the question. On the other hand, requiring a special majority (more than 50 per cent plus 1) for secession would depart from precedents since all past Canadian referendums, as well as the two referendums necessary to bring Newfoundland into Confederation, have been held on the basis of the simple majority rule. Any attempt to impose a higher threshold would run into insuperable difficulties, as the choice of any number larger than 50 per cent would appear to be entirely arbitrary.

The best way to make sure that the will of a majority of Quebecers has been clearly expressed is to hold a second referendum once the results of negotiations between Quebec and the rest of Canada on the terms of secession are known. Voters will then be able to evaluate the true consequences of secession on matters like Canadian citizenship, the Canadian dollar, the proportion of the public debt of Canada to be assumed by Quebec, the economic or political ties maintained with Canada, as well as the territorial integrity of Quebec. This time, voters will be very aware of all the difficulties and disruptions that may be caused by secession, as it must be assumed that ROC representatives will have stressed them amply during the period of negotiations. Therefore, if the second referendum is also positive, the will of Quebec voters will have to be considered as sufficiently clear.

For legal scholars, the most remarkable aspect of the ruling is how the Court has answered all the questions without ever referring to the actual specific provisions of the Constitution. This case admirably illustrates the considerable margin of freedom a supreme or constitutional court can exercise in applying the Constitution, by submitting the express content of the instrument to its implied principles. The whole judgement is based strictly on four general principles that are today present in every democratic, liberal and federal constitutional system in the world. These are the democratic principle, which gives Quebecers the right to decide their own political future and grounds the obligation of the rest of Canada to negotiate a secession approved by a clear majority on a clear question; the federal principle, which forms the basis of the obligation of Quebec to negotiate with its federation partners the rupture of a union existing for more than 131 years; the protection of minorities, which asks for respect of minority rights in the conduct as well as in the outcome of negotiations; and, finally, the rule of law and the principle of constitutionalism, which demand that secession of a province be achieved within the existing constitutional framework.

Ironically, if the Court had decided the *Patriation Reference* in 1981 and the *Quebec Veto Reference* in 1982 by applying the same four principles, it never could have arrived at the answers actually given in these two cases. The federal principle would not have allowed it to pronounce the legality of a major constitutional reform to which only two provinces had consented at that time, and the protection of minorities would have prevented it from ruling that the nine English-speaking provinces and the federal authorities, controlled by an English-speaking majority, could impose the same kind of constitutional change on the only province where francophones form the majority. The 1982 patriation did not respect the rights of the most important minority in Canada, the francophones, 90 per cent of whom live in Quebec.

12

The Secession Reference and Constitutional Paradox

John D. Whyte

John D. Whyte is Professor of Law at Queen's University and Deputy Attorney General and Deputy Minister of Justice for Saskatchewan. He served as co-counsel for the Intervenor, the Attorney General of Saskatchewan, in the Quebec Secession Reference.

In the portion of his factum dealing with the first question addressed to the Supreme Court (whether Quebec can effect unilateral secession from Canada under the Constitution), the Attorney General of Saskatchewan speculated on the political conditions and processes necessary for an amendment to the Constitution. In these paragraphs, he identified as conditions a clear expression of support for independence in Quebec expressed through a referendum; some expression of the national will to negotiate with Quebec; and negotiated terms of separation touching on such things as assets, debt, borders, rights of minority communities, citizenship, monetary matters, pensions, rights of office holders, and so forth.

This section of the factum is explicitly disconnected from arguments on the content of the constitutional order. It was not meant to answer the question of what our constitutional rule for secession is, but rather to show that constitutional rules operate in political contexts and that their normative effect is determined by their relevance to those contexts. Saskatchewan was, in short, reassuring the Court that the rules it prescribed could well bear on political developments around a secession initiative. The factum also recognized that constitutional rules might be irrelevant to those developments. The Saskatchewan factum was meant to be a partial answer to those many voices saying that the Constitutional Reference was a mistake because the birth and dissolution of nations are not amenable to legal norms. It said, in short, "Maybe yes, maybe no, but we are not free to prejudge the weight of law on politics."

The factum proceeded from an assumption about law and political legitimacy: that we cannot always measure the legitimacy of high-stakes national politics in terms of whether that politics sustains the integrity of what has gone before. It is clear that American constitutional commentators (notably Bob Cover and Bruce Ackerman) see national politics as more closely connected to the constitutional order. For them, the constitution establishes a national narrative that at the same time enables social and legal transformation and suppresses or outflanks revolution; generates new normative communities and constantly expresses fidelity to original commitments and structures. The Canadian sense of constitutionalism, as represented in the factum, does not go this far in embracing the political order — it seeks to express less of our political culture and accepts the strange fact that, even in a nation governed by constitutionalism, politics does not necessarily engage law.

There is another way that I would put this. If we do have an organic sense of our nation, our Constitution is not a powerful site of that organic understanding. We do not think that the transformative effect of nation-creating on the identities of Canada's parts and its people is captured in the Constitution or through constitutional law. It is not in the constitutional order that the intellectual basis for our nationalism is expressed. It is not in the Constitution, or in its application, that the national virtues are enumerated and tied to basic structures and arrangements. For Canada, the organic nation is an expression of commerce or transportation or, for example, is to be seen in the discovery by the National Museum's Marius Barbeau of Emily Carr and his connecting her to a developing indigenous artistic sensibility — in short, it is a consequence of a life lived together.[1]

The Saskatchewan factum, then, although in other parts supportive of an organic understanding of nation, adopts a view of constitutional order that is modest, limited and contingent — contingent on ideas of political legitimacy and political identity that likely have an origin elsewhere and whose vitality is renewed not through honouring our Constitution but through other, barely seen and understood, processes flowing, perhaps, from the PMO, or from centres of influence on Front Street West (whether the CBC or *The Globe and Mail*).

From one perspective, the Supreme Court of Canada in the Secession Reference would have none of this modesty. Consider paragraph 69. This paragraph concludes the Court's reflections on the constitutional principle of democracy. The Court states:

> The *Constitution Act, 1982* gives expression to this principle, by conferring a right to initiate constitutional change on each participant in Confederation. In our view, the existence of this right imposes a corresponding duty on the participants in Confederation to engage in constitutional discussions in order to acknowledge and address democratic expressions of a desire for change on other provinces.

The Court in these two sentences leaves behind the careful distancing of law from political legitimacy that has marked Canadian constitutionalism. This is not to say that this shift is unfortunate or mistaken. The political role of constitutionalism, especially since it has been a narrow role, is not fixed. As David Schneiderman has pointed out, our constitutionalism was, for a long time, focused on maintaining structures conducive to energetic economic development, albeit, perhaps, as an adjunct to national development. It could well be time to adopt a larger state project for constitutionalism —the project of measuring political legitimacy.

But there is a strange twist to this expansion of the Constitution's purview. The Court claims a role for the Constitution in the politics of Canada's dissolution, but it also creates a high order of constitutional recognition for expressions of provincial self-determination. This recognition stands in stark contrast to two claims made by those who have used legal arguments to resist Quebec's secession. The first is that a Quebec vote for independence is legally meaningless and triggers no consequence and no duty. The second is that Canada, as an organic state, cannot be dismantled (apart from circumstances of the widest possible national concurrence) and that it is the right of a Canadian majority to insist on maintaining the integrity of the state.

What has produced the Court's dissent from these legal orthodoxies is the recognition that it is politically unrealistic to claim that such strong propositions can be factored into our constitutional law. The Court's own, more modest, factoring process — its attempt to bridge constitutional principle with politics — is not, however, particularly convincing. The Court pulled the duty to negotiate out of rarefied air. There is nothing in the democratic principle (claimed to be the basis of the duty to negotiate) that allows it to "trump" other more fundamental constitutional ideas. In fact, the Court sets an extremely simple or direct form of democratic expression above the multi-layered understanding of democracy that is actually required to co-ordinate the democratic principle with constitutionalism.

Furthermore, the Court's lack of legal commitment is also found in its unconvincing and inconsistently expressed claim of the blanket non-justiciability of all issues with respect to the essential legal requirements in the process leading to secession — legal requirements that will bind the parties to a secession arrangement but, evidently, are not subject to adjudication or enforcement by the courts. The Court's connection of constitutional principle to the politics of extreme choices, and its disconnection of constitutional principle from the rule of law's chief instrumentalities, reveals a remarkable shift toward constitutionalism as a passive marker of political legitimacy. The Court believes that its role is to reveal constraints on the politics of dissolving a nation by putting in place certain moral demarcations. No doubt, the Court is driven to the position that the Constitution addresses the whole of the dissolution process but controls none of it, because it feels this is the only effective role open to it — simply to identify what conduct is legitimate in a unique Canadian historical moment and what conduct is not, and hope that the protagonists believe that legitimacy matters. The Court's position is that legitimacy matters, both in amending the Constitution and in winning international recognition, and, as a practical political matter, that legitimate conduct is the only way for secession to succeed, as well as the only way for it to be successfully averted.

What can one say about this calculation about the role for constitutional law? One might say it lacks conviction. It is based on the twin beliefs that our Constitution contains a complex moral vision of rights and entitlements and respect for individuals, communities, branches and jurisdictions, and this moral vision provides a constitutional chart for appropriate legal behaviour. The judgement is not, however, based on the idea that the Court's sense of constitutional meaning should be accepted as the nation's sense of constitutional meaning. From some perspectives — an American perspective, for instance — this acceptance is an unthinkable concession to the political branches. It reveals to us, I think, that our

Court is willing to subscribe to a less mature idea of Canadian constitutional democracy than was embedded in our political culture prior to the Charter of Rights — or is it prior to Quebec's quest for independence? (In this paper, I cannot begin to trace the origins of our changed constitutionalism. However, my sense is that it is less a result of introducing an individual and group rights agenda in the Constitution through the Charter than the long-term effective questioning by Quebec of the reality of Canada's organic nationalism.)

The Court's decision not only reveals a particular conception of constitutionalism, it reveals a conception of nation. The paradox is that normally one would think that belief in a rich, substantive national constitutionalism — one, for instance, that contains elaborate ideas about political and cultural communities and their interrelationship — would go hand in hand with a strong sense of nation: of national identity and national integrity. Of course, it may not be an accurate inference from the Court's holding that there is a constitutional duty to at least negotiate about national dissolution that it has adopted a thin view of the Canadian nation. In fact, in referring to the words of George-Etienne Cartier, the Court has deepened and historicized the conception of the Canadian federation to present it as generative of a new political entity, all of whose members could claim to participate in its fundamental reformation. The Court quotes Cartier's view that "[w]hen we are united together...we shall form a political nationality with which neither the national origin, nor the religion of any individual will interfere." Cartier, while insisting on the Confederation promise that the founding nations of Canada would not be forced into assimilation, went on to say:

> In our own Federation, we will have Catholic and Protestant, English, French, Irish and Scotch, each by his efforts and his success will increase prosperity and glory of the new Confederation. We are of different races, not for the purpose of warring against each other, but in order to complete and emulate for the general welfare (para. 43).

The Court did not take from this passage, however, the moral notion that there has been built a new nation from which, in fairness to all those who contributed, whether through economic integration, building national transportation systems or art criticism, there can be no turning back. The Court chose to focus first on the accommodation of diversity. But the Court did end its reflection on Cartier with the much diluted sentiment that Canada is "a unified and independent political state in which different peoples could resolve their disagreements and work together toward common goals and a common interest."

The result of the Reference, however, clearly avoids the strong version of the organic state whose integrity can be compromised only in truly exceptional circumstances. The Court placed the Canadian nation somewhere between a compact of states and Lincoln's view of the nation as a "perpetual union." It chose a middle course to capture the idea of nation in Canada. It recognized a constitutional barrier to unilateral secession *and* a constitutional requirement on the nation as a whole to conduct negotiations with a single province seeking to effect secession from the nation. This is not an idea of nation that stirs loyalty anywhere. Is it, however, the right idea of the Canadian nation?s

For one thing, this level of constitutional commitment to national integrity may well be a good match with Canada's actual constitutional history. No prior version of the Canadian colony or nation has been considered immutable. The change from free colony to self-governing colony, from constituent part of the British Empire to national autonomy, from attachment through several residual British roles to attainment of full sovereignty, has occurred relatively easily and without reference to the organic quality of these arrangements.

At the level of national romanticism, there are some who argue that a nation is not likely to have an organic sense of itself unless it has arisen in war: unless it is forged through the transformation represented by the movement from personal death to the birth of a nation. On the other hand, endless numbers of Canadian nationalists have seen the pattern of sacrifices, sharing and cross-fertilization in Canada as being constitutive of a nation whose integrity has pre-eminent value.

In contrast, the Court's view may represent the modern conception of nation as an arrangement of market convenience whose role has been seriously diminished. It may feel that it is futile to cling to national integrity when the role of the modern state is so attenuated.

Whatever the Court's deep thinking was behind its invention of the duty to negotiate, it has generated a view of the state as susceptible to fundamental changes in order better to reflect the needs, interests and identities of its component parts. Perhaps this is the sane way for all nations to see themselves. It may be the view that forestalls bloodshed. However, it does not sound a note of confidence in the viability of pluralistic states. In that way, the vision of nation implicit in the judgement may not be the least bit modern.

13

Quebec Secession and Aboriginal Peoples: Important Signals from the Supreme Court

Paul Joffe

This article originally appeared in Canada Watch *in February, 1999 (Vol. 7, no. 1). Paul Joffe is a member of the Quebec and Ontario bars. He was part of the legal team acting on behalf of the Intervener Grand Council of the Crees in the Quebec Secession Reference.*

The interpretations and rulings of the Supreme Court of Canada in the Quebec Secession Reference should prove to be of far-reaching significance for aboriginal peoples. In particular, the aboriginal dimensions have extensive implications for Quebec's sovereignty project.

While the judgement includes a few key pronouncements specifically relating to aboriginal peoples, the Court indicated that it was not necessary to explore further in this reference their rights and concerns. The Court took this position only because it had concluded that there is no right to unilateral secession by Quebec authorities under Canadian or international law (para. 139).

Since the judgement expressly highlights the importance of aboriginal peoples' rights and concerns, it would be erroneous to presume that the judgement can be properly analysed solely in federal–provincial or non-aboriginal terms. As described below, there are compelling signals from the Supreme Court that should shape developments in the future.

Prior to examining the aboriginal aspects of the judgement, it is important to raise a preliminary, overarching concern. On the day after the Supreme Court rendered this historic judgement, Premier Lucien Bouchard emphasized in televised interviews that the rest of Canada would be constitutionally bound to negotiate with Quebec following a successful referendum. At the same time, he declared that the Quebec government is not bound by the Court's judgement. Such a view creates an unworkable double standard. A future Quebec referendum on secession could only acquire legitimacy, as set out in the judgement, if the Quebec government first accepts that it is bound, like all other political actors in Canada, by all aspects of the judgement. Otherwise, from the outset, there would be no common legal and constitutional framework for any secessionist project.

In regard to Quebec's sovereignty project, I would like to list a number of aspects in the Court's judgement that appear vital for aboriginal peoples. These points serve to balance legality and legitimacy. They also give rise to principles and norms that reflect the importance of dignity, equality and mutual respect for all peoples in Canada. Many of the points summarized below go well beyond aboriginal peoples in their scope and significance, both for the present and the long term.

1. **Unilateral secession is not ruled out**. As a result of the Supreme Court judgement, the threat of unilateral secession by Quebec is not totally eliminated. *De facto* secession (paras. 142, 155) could still be attempted by Quebec in the future. However, the likelihood of unilateral action in the next few years has been considerably diminished, to the advantage of aboriginal peoples, among others, in Canada.

2. **Increased importance is placed on clarity**. In terms of clarifying the rules for any secession project, the Court's judgement goes beyond requiring in the future a clear referendum question on secession and a clear majority vote. Unlike the situation that prevailed during the 1995 referendum on Quebec secession, there are now a number of judicial interpretations, criteria and rules arising from the Court's decision, by which to measure the alleged validity or legitimacy of any party's position. Increased clarity and transparency should be the result.

3. **Claims to legitimacy are all relative**. The Court's judgement makes clear that legitimacy is a relative concept (para. 66).

Following any successful referendum in the future, the legitimacy claims of Quebecers must still be balanced by the legitimacies, rights and interests validly asserted by others. Therefore, should the Quebec government seek to deny the legitimacy and rights of aboriginal peoples to determine their own future, then any claim of legitimacy by the Quebec government would itself be severely undermined.

4. **The democratic principle is applicable to all.** The democratic principle is not limited to Quebecers clearly expressing their collective will through a referendum. The Court's judgement stipulates that the rights, obligations and legitimate aspirations of everyone in must be reconciled (para. 104). Therefore, in the Quebec secession context, should aboriginal peoples express their own collective will through their own referendums or other democratic means, these legitimate and democratic voices must be accorded equal recognition, consideration and respect without discrimination or other double standard.

   Neither Canadian nor international law recognizes any doctrine of superiority of one people over another. As the preamble of the International Convention on the Elimination of All Forms of Racial Discrimination provides, "... any doctrine of superiority based on racial differentiation is scientifically false, morally condemnable, socially unjust and dangerous."

5. **Aboriginal peoples are not simply minorities.** The judgement generally includes aboriginal peoples under the constitutional principle of "protection of minorities"(para. 82). This does not mean that the Court intended to imply that aboriginal peoples are simply "minorities." In the 1996 case of *R. v. Van der Peet*, Chief Justice Lamer, on behalf of the majority, emphasized the original occupation of North America by aboriginal peoples and then stated: "It is this fact, and this fact above all others, which separates Aboriginal peoples from all other minority groups in Canadian society and which mandates their special legal, and now constitutional, status."

6. **Federal and provincial governments are not the sole partici-pants in future secession negotiations.** In terms of who has a role in the political aspects of any future secession process, the Court refers generally to "political actors" (paras. 98, 100, 101, 110, 153). In some instances, federal and provincial governments are mentioned (para. 86), but it cannot be concluded that they are the only "political actors" involved. "Participants" *other than*

federal and provincial governments are expressly contemplated by the Court for any future secession negotiations (para. 92).

It is clear that, for secession and other constitutional purposes, aboriginal peoples are distinct "political actors" in Canada. Section 35.1 of the Constitution Act, 1982 expressly provides for the direct involvement of representatives of the aboriginal peoples in First Ministers' conferences whenever amendments are contemplated to section 35 and other constitutional provisions pertaining to them. Also, the established practice in Canada is to include the representatives of aboriginal peoples in constitutional negotiations as distinct "political actors."

7. **The number of "peoples" in Quebec is not defined.** The Court chose not to answer the question of who constitute "peoples" in Quebec for purposes of self-determination under international law. However, it indicated that the characteristics of a "people" include a common language and culture (para. 125). These criteria suggest that the Court is not heading toward any definition of a single "people" in Quebec, based simply on provincial territorial considerations.

In regard to aboriginal peoples in Quebec, their cultures and spirituality are not those of Quebecers. Each aboriginal people has its own way of life. Each clearly chooses to identify itself as a distinct people. While French Canadians in Quebec are likely to constitute "a people" for purposes of self-determination, there is no principle of Canadian or international law that would compel aboriginal peoples against their will to identify as one people with Quebecers.

8. **The right to self-determination is part of Canadian law.** The judgement states that "the existence of the right of a people to self-determination is now so widely recognized in international conventions that the principle has acquired a status beyond 'convention' and is considered a general principle of international law" (para. 114).

The term "general principle of international law" is highly significant. According to international jurists, this term refers to customary international law. The term may also overlap with other principles. However, the sentence and overall context in which the Supreme Court used the term, as well as the references cited on this point in the judgement, lead to the conclusion that the Court was describing the right to self-determination as nothing less than customary international law.

Canadian case law suggests that norms of customary international law are "adopted" directly into Canadian domestic law, without any need for the incorporation of these standards by statute. This is true, as long as there is no conflict with statutory law or well-established rules of the common law. In this way, the right to self-determination can be said to be a part of the internal law of Canada. This has far-reaching positive implications that go beyond the context of Quebec's secession — implications that would hold for any aboriginal people who demonstrates that it is "a people" under international law.

9. **Boundary issues must be addressed in negotiations.** The issue of Quebec's boundaries is not only underlined by the Court in terms of Canada's "national existence" (para. 96), but also in regard to aboriginal peoples — especially their "northern lands" (para. 139). In conformity with the judgement, boundary issues must be addressed in any negotiations on Quebec's secession.

Moreover, the Court adds that "none of the rights or principles under discussion is absolute to the exclusion of others" (para. 93). Therefore, the Quebec government could not rely on constitutional guarantees for its present provincial boundaries to prevent division of the province in the event of secession. Since Canada and Quebec would both be divisible in secession negotiations, the Quebec government could not insist that the international law principle of *uti possidetis* must prevail to conserve the province's current boundaries.

10. **Constitutional amendment procedures are not absolute.** The Court states that underlying constitutional principles, such as democracy and protection of minorities, apply to more than secession negotiations (paras. 93–95). These principles "animate the whole of our Constitution" (paras. 148, 32) including the "amendment process" (para. 92). This suggests that the express provisions to amend the Constitution of Canada are qualified by unwritten principles and are not absolute.

In an extreme situation such as secession, the underlying constitutional principles could serve to limit the express powers of federal and provincial legislatures. Should legislatures violate the principle of democracy in relation to aboriginal peoples, the courts could rule that the amendment procedures used to allow Quebec secession were "not in accordance with the authority contained in the Constitution of Canada" (Constitution Act, 1982, section 52(3)).

As the above ten points illustrate, the question of legitimacy of Quebec secession is inextricably tied to the respect accorded to the rights, legitimacies and aspirations of aboriginal peoples, among others. Non-aboriginal governments and legislatures in Canada do not have the discretion to determine the future of aboriginal peoples. This is fortified by the fact that the Canadian system of government has been "transformed to a significant extent from a system of Parliamentary supremacy to one of constitutional supremacy" (para. 72).

The status and rights of aboriginal peoples are fundamental elements in Canada's Constitution. Protection of these rights "reflects an important underlying constitutional value" (para. 82). Should a successful referendum in Quebec lead to secession negotiations in the future, the Court's judgement has strengthened the position of aboriginal peoples in Quebec to make their own collective choices, participate directly in negotiations, and assert their basic rights. As the Court stipulates in the Secession Reference, any future negotiations on Quebec secession must be "principled" (paras. 104, 106, 149).

In particular, the human right of aboriginal peoples to self-determination militates against their forcible inclusion in any seceding Quebec should such a process be initiated in the future. In regard to the James Bay and Northern Quebec Agreement, the right to self-determination of the Crees and Inuit reinforces the fact that any alteration of their constitutionally protected treaty rights requires their free and informed consent.

While clearly there are no guarantees, the Quebec government may ultimately be able to negotiate an independent Quebec state. However, consistent with principles of fairness, democracy and respect for human rights, this would not necessarily include the vast northern and other aboriginal traditional territories currently in Quebec.

The Constitutional Obligation to Negotiate

Alan C. Cairns

Alan Cairns is the John T. Saywell Professor of Political Science, York University. This essay is abridged from the original, which appeared in Constitutional Forum constitutionnel *10 (1998): 26-30.*

The *Globe and Mail* headline "The Quebec Ruling: Canada Must Negotiate after Yes Vote" correctly identified the most innovative aspect of the Supreme Court's ruling. According to Conservative senator and constitutional law professor Gerald Beaudoin, "[t]he constitutional obligation to negotiate that's new in the jurisprudence ... I am very impressed — that's quite something."[1] Premier Bouchard loudly proclaimed the obligation to negotiate as a victory for the sovereignists. It blunted the federalist assertion that Ottawa could not or would not negotiate following a Yes vote. "The obligation to negotiate," asserted Bouchard, "has a constitutional status. This is of the utmost importance. There is no way the federal government could escape it." Subsequently, extracting even more positive results from the decision, he asserted that Canada will have "no choice but to negotiate a new economic relationship with Quebec."[2]

The Court's finding of an obligation to negotiate, the linchpin of its analysis once it had decided that neither domestic constitutional law nor international law authorized the unilateral secession of Quebec from Canada, deserves intense scrutiny. While the Court's dictum on the obligation to negotiate has injected a welcome note of civility into our constitutional introspection, the analysis that supports it and the consequences that might flow from it have serious weaknesses....

The Court appears to propose two competing negotiating/amending processes. On the one hand, much of its analysis presupposes the use of the basic amending formulas of the 1982 *Constitution Act*, which privilege governments and legislatures. The decision speaks of the legal necessity of "an amendment to the Constitution" (para. 84) and states that secession "must be undertaken pursuant to the Constitution of Canada" (para. 104). Elsewhere, however, the decision asserts that negotiations would "require the reconciliation of various rights and obligations by the representatives of two legitimate majorities, namely, the clear majority of the population of Quebec, and the clear majority of Canada as a whole, *whatever that may be*" (para. 93, emphasis added). Are these two ways of describing the same process, with the latter being the Court's interpretation of the former? Or are these two different processes? Claude Ryan has interpreted these as two processes, although he castigated the Court for its lack of clarity on this key issue.[3] The two majorities are dissimilar, as one refers to population and the other refers to Canada as a whole. The meaning of "representatives of [...] the clear majority of Canada as a whole" is unclear, as the Court intimated with its phrase "whatever that may be." Clear majority does, however, appear to rule out unanimity as a requirement, in which case the Court has eliminated one of the amending formulas that elsewhere it had said were not up for judicial determination at this time (para. 105). On the other hand, "clear majority" is not a particularly helpful way to describe the 7/50 process that requires the approval of eight of the eleven governments — the federal government and seven provinces with 50% of the population. It is even less appropriate as a description of the degree of agreement required to get over the hurdles of the federal government's 1996 loan of its veto to the five regions of Canada.

The Court's description of one of the two negotiating parties as "Canada as a whole" raises more complicated problems. Canada as a whole necessarily includes Quebec. Accordingly, Quebec participates twice — once on its own behalf as a secession-seeking government and also as part of "the clear majority of Canada as a whole," which necessarily includes the federal government representing all Canadians, including Quebecers. By contrast, there is no mention of the rest of Canada — the prospective new Canada[4] — in the judgement, even by inference. The premise appears to be that Quebec is cleanly excised, and "Canada" continues. However, new Canada with Quebec gone is a new country, in a way that Canada without P.E.I. would not be. It is not simply a slightly modified version of the old Canada. To suggest that it is, is to argue that Quebec's presence has had only minimal influence on Canada's evolution as a people, on the federal system, on our foreign policy, etc. Accordingly, the processes for negotiating and reaching a constitutionalized secession agreement need to accommodate a successor new Canada that will no longer be a whole, but a smaller Canada with a gaping hole in the middle. This Canada is the second new country that will emerge should Quebec leave, and it is the country to which all the arrangements struck with Quebec will apply.

The Court unavoidably and unsurprisingly advocates a lead role for the Canadian government in the negotiation process. Such a lead role for the federal government is justified by the gravity of the issue, the threatened dismemberment of the country; by the fact that the federal government has moral obligations to Quebecers who do not wish to leave Canada and to those who are concerned with their position in an independent Quebec; by its fiduciary obligations to native peoples; and by the fact that implementing secession will require an incredibly complex devolution of federal responsibilities in Quebec to the new seceding government — including offices, hundreds of thousands of files and records, the proffering of policy advice to the new administrative class, and the movement of civil service personnel in both directions — all of which, without federal government support, will degenerate into chaos. A lead role for the federal government is further required because Canada continues to exist, and it remains the government of all Canadians until Quebec's exit is formalized by a constitutional amendment or by a successful unilateral secession. Further, negotiations may fail, an unconstitutional secession may not be attempted, and Canada may continue. Or, in the post-Yes negotiations, the federal government, supported by provincial governments, may manage to keep Canada together by an acceptable offer of renewed federalism at one minute to midnight. Whether Quebec goes or stays, all of the preceding scenarios necessitate a prominent, leading role for the federal government in the post-Yes negotiations. Further, whatever amending formula is required, the legislative approval of the federal government is necessary. These are heavy responsibilities that reasonably belong to the federal government (with, of course, significant input from provincial governments and probably from nongovernmental actors). They are the daunting tidying-up problems of disentanglement, moral obligations that properly pertain to the federal government, and a possible last-ditch effort to keep the country together and preserve the federal government's coast-to-coast role. The responsibility to represent the interests of new Canada, however, or even of its future central government, does not logically apply to the federal government of old Canada, even in combination with provincial governments.

Given a clear question, a clear Quebec majority, the constitutional obligations on both sides to negotiate, the possibility that negotiations might be successful, or the possibility of unilateral secession should negotiations fail, old Canada might not survive. If and when that happens, a process directed to the secession of Quebec will have produced two new countries, not one. At this point, Canada as a whole, in the language of the Supreme Court, ceases to exist. The federal government of old Canada also ceases to exist. The agreement it has struck, assuming a constitutional exit, applies not to itself but to its successor, a shrunken survivor, the retreating central government of a fragmented, different country, probably still called Canada. Whether new Canada survives as a united country or experiences further fragmentation is debatable. In any case, the answer to that question may not immediately emerge. As is argued elsewhere, new Canada will emerge as a separate state with virtually no preparation, either of governments or of citizens, for its new status. Given that lack of preparation, the rational course of action is for the new, smaller Canada to continue with its existing constitutional arrangements — modified only by the excision of Quebec — while it works out its own future.

The difficulties confronting the new Canada will be compounded if the Supreme Court's interpretation of the negotiating task is accepted, for the agreements it will be expected to assume will have been bargained by others in its absence. It will be the recipient of decisions made by an entity — Canada as a whole — that will have disappeared from the scene. Canada as a whole, for example, may agree to reciprocal regimes of official minority language rights far more generous than would be voluntarily assumed by the successor, new Canada.

The emergence of a new country — the new Canada — is of no concern to the Court. The Court's task was to examine the legalities of unilateral secession by Quebec. However, the secession of Quebec creates not one, but two new states — new Canada and Quebec —

a reality the Court could not address or even perceive, given the questions it was asked. Only one of those prospective states is present at the bargaining table that leads to its creation; new Canada emerges as a by-product of negotiations by old Canada to work out the terms for the secession of Quebec. Quebec will automatically be a player in its own emergence. However, in the Court's interpretation of the post-Yes negotiation scenario, no one speaks for the new Canada. It is not there.

Overcoming the discrepancy between the bargaining objectives of old Canada and a prospective new Canada requires the explicit recognition that the secession of Quebec will create two new states, not one, and that a process designed only to work out the secession of Quebec is unacceptable. Further, any idea that the federal government of old Canada can speak and bargain for its successor, the central government of a different successor country, should be rejected. Indeed, the Court's decision makes it clear that the federal government speaks for all Canadians inside and outside Quebec until secession is an accomplished fact; it cannot simultaneously be a proxy for new Canada — for Canada without Quebec — particularly if, as may be the case, it is tempted to make last-ditch efforts to placate Quebec by explicit major proposals for renewed federalism. The idea that the governments of the provinces in negotiations focusing on the secession of Quebec can be trusted to represent the interests of a prospective Canada without Quebec is also implausible, unless that future country is to be thought of as an aggregation of particularisms.

Canada without Quebec (new Canada) and Canada as a whole with Quebec (old Canada) are clearly different constellations of interests. They would strike somewhat dissimilar deals with Quebec. Accordingly, a deal struck by Canada as a whole may subsequently be unacceptable to the shrunken new Canada, the former ROC. Given this fact, the Supreme Court either seriously misunderstood or ignored the complexity of the negotiation process it was recommending. Its proposals were directed to the emergence of one new state. It overlooked the simultaneous emergence of a second state — a smaller, new Canada — and thus left the latter in the audience, absent at its own creation. It addressed itself to the task of establishing guidelines for the conciliation of the concerns of "the clear majority of the population of Quebec, and the clear majority of Canada as a whole," but not to the concerns of any kind of majority from the emerging second state....

By focusing on old Canada bargaining with Quebec over the terms of secession, the Court neglects what will be left behind following Quebec's surgical removal. The magnitude of the change is minimized by the constant resort to "Canada" and by the failure or unwillingness to employ any label to distinguish new Canada (without Quebec) from old Canada (with Quebec). This exaggerates the continuity between the (old) Canada that precedes Quebec's secession and the (new) Canada that follows it. This might be acceptable if the seceding province was small and on the geographic periphery. It is misleading when the seceding province is Quebec, whose location, numbers and history made it central to the nature of old Canada, and whose departure would correspondingly be a major shock. New Canada, therefore, is not simply old Canada writ small....

Apparently the Court thought that negotiating a response to a Quebec Yes was a question of "will," which could be resolved by underlining the constitutional obligation to negotiate secession terms in appropriate circumstances. It is also, however, a question of capacity, which becomes the question of how a negotiating process and an amending formula that assumes constitutional continuity can be employed to generate two new independent states. The Court's attention focused exclusively on Quebec and completely neglected new Canada. The Court's negotiation proposal, therefore, is incomplete. It only does half the job.

It would be unfair to affix too much of the blame for this shortcoming on the Court itself. Its answers were structured by the questions it was asked. The justices focused on the legality of the unilateral secession of Quebec as part of the Plan B strategy to inform Quebecers that secession was a high-risk enterprise. By suggesting criteria that must be met in the referendum process — a clear question and a clear majority followed by a constitutionally obligatory negotiating process characterized by good faith on both sides — the Court has removed some of the risk, for all parties. The Court, however, doubtless unwittingly, has also structured the post-Yes negotiation process in such a way that a new set of risks has been visited on the second successor country that will emerge should Quebec leave. This appears as a classic example of the unintended consequence of purposive social action, one that the federal government did not foresee when it launched the reference, one the Court did not intend, one no provincial government publicly anticipated, and, at the time of writing, one that no post-decision commentator appears to have noted. It is not too late to supplement the Court's contributions by devising a negotiating process that is appropriate to the actual tasks that will confront the post-Yes negotiators.

What if Quebecers Voted Clearly for Secession?

Claude Ryan

———————

This article by Claude Ryan, former leader of the Quebec Liberal Party, appeared in The Globe and Mail *on 27 August 1998.*

In good logic, one cannot subscribe at the same time to a given proposition and to its opposite. When Jean Chrétien and Lucien Bouchard both proclaimed that their respective positions had been enhanced by the Supreme Court's ruling on the secession of Quebec, I undertook a second, more critical reading of the Court's opinion.

While my enthusiasm over the passages dealing with the broad principles defined by the Court remains high, I must confess to a real concern about the way the Court applied those principles to the Quebec case. My difficulties are with the core issue of what should happen after a referendum in which a clear majority of Quebecers opted for sovereignty.

Let us first deal with the period preceding a referendum. As long as Quebec remains a province of Canada, its legislature and government must act in conformity with the Constitution, including its underlying principles, which the Court enunciated with impressive clarity. Although Quebec did not subscribe to the 1982 Constitution, it is bound by its provisions, including the amending formula which is omnipresent, though mentioned explicitly only once, in the Court's ruling. Any action by the Quebec government that would contravene the Constitution would be inadmissible and could be countered by appropriate means.

From this perspective, Mr. Bouchard should attach more importance than he appears willing to do to the Court's advice that, to be acceptable, a future referendum must be held around a clear question. The wording of the question must remain the prerogative of the National Assembly; but in view of the vast web of rights and obligations created by more than a century of shared existence with Quebec, the rest of Canada would also have an undeniable interest in the decision. From the standpoint of federal courtesy and sheer political realism, the views of other governments should be received with respect. To turn a deaf ear to such views in the name of Quebec democracy would be to ignore the federal principle which, according to the Court, is a major pillar of our constitutional system.

The same considerations must apply to the debate about what would constitute an acceptable majority in a referendum on the future of Quebec. One cannot rule out *a priori* the advantages of classic majority rule. But simple majority rule must not necessarily be the last word in a matter of this importance. As the Court aptly recalled, there are many examples in our system of government of decisions that cannot be made on the basis of a simple majority vote. The rights of minorities in particular would be at the mercy of the least change in the direction of political winds if they were to be adjudicated solely by simple majority rule. Not only Mr. Chrétien but also many Quebecers consider that other avenues could also be explored. Why should their views be cavalierly ignored without any discussion?

The main difficulty with the Court's ruling, in my view, is in its perception of what would result from a clear vote for sovereignty. The Court had to decide whether an unprecedented situation requiring an equally novel approach would thus have been created, or whether the new situation should be dealt with simply by resorting to existing rules. Its approach was, to say the least, ambivalent.

On the one hand, it clearly recommended that other governments enter into sincere negotiations with the Quebec government with a view to arriving at a mutually acceptable settlement of the many problems that must be resolved before secession can take place. It added that the ensuing negotiations would "require the reconciliation of various rights and interests by *the representatives of two legitimate majorities*, namely, the clear majority of the population of Quebec, and the clear majority of Canada as a whole, whatever that may be [emphasis added]." It even concluded, "There can be no suggestion that either of those two majorities 'trumps' the other" (para. 93).

On the other hand, the Court strongly affirmed that "any attempt to effect the separation of a province from Canada must be undertaken *pursuant to the Constitution of Canada*" (para. 104) [emphasis added]. Unless I am mistaken, this implies that any constitutional modification aimed at allowing the secession of Quebec would have to be approved under the existing amending formula or under another formula that would require the unanimous consent of Parliament and all the provinces.

How is the paragraph suggesting negotiations between "the *representatives of two legitimate majorities*" to be reconciled with the many passages in which the Court affirms that the amendment of the Constitution begins with a political process undertaken *pursuant to the Constitution itself* [emphasis added]? Would there be two bargaining tables, one political but without any legal clout, the other legal but having little if any political clout with one of the two "legitimate majorities"? What would the standing be of the parties at those tables? Who would have the power to decide? How would effective decisions be reached?

The Court failed to clarify these points. Unless they were resolved to the satisfaction of the "two legitimate majorities" in advance of negotiations, a large cloud of uncertainty would hang over the exercise even before it began. If the last word were to emanate from the legal table, how could Quebec be expected to forget that, under the same amending formula that would presumably continue to apply, two provinces representing less than 5% of the population of Canada had enough power in 1990 to block the passage of the Meech Lake Accord?

Under those conditions, the possibility of an impasse in the negotiations would be dangerously real. Should an impasse arise, the Court warns us — rather summarily, in my view — that it would be of no help. "We need not speculate here," it writes nonchalantly, "as to what would then transpire. Under the Constitution, secession requires that an amendment be negotiated" (para. 97). Does this mean that an amending formula that was not conceived to deal with a case of secession and was never accepted by Quebec must be the ultimate legal instrument for the adoption or the rejection of a decision authorizing the secession of Quebec? Quebec, if negotiations were to abort or if a veto were to block a settlement negotiated in good faith, would have no other option but to either renounce its project of sovereignty or pursue it by extra-constitutional means.

In the latter case, international opinion might be influenced, as the Court says, by unjustified denial of Quebec's right to self-determination. But Quebec, in embarking on that course, would engage in a risky operation in which most advantages would be on the other side. The Court spoke of an obligation to negotiate that would be incumbent on all governments. Should the other governments refuse to engage in meaningful negotiations, the Court had no other remedy to propose to Quebec than docile resignation within the existing constitutional order or the unpredictable adventure of extra-constitutional secession.

* * *

In the light of this interpretation, which I hope will be proven wrong, one can better understand the triumphant tone adopted by Mr. Chrétien in his comments on the Supreme Court's ruling. While bound in a very general way by the broad principles defined by the Court, the federal government, if negotiations with Quebec around secession became necessary, would control most of the major cards that might affect the outcome of the negotiations — in particular, a larger population, the inherent rigidities of the Constitution, superior force and a stronger bargaining position in the international arena. In the event of a winning referendum, Quebec might well win a battle of principles but lose the decision. The foreseeable price on both sides would be sour rancour, increased suspicion and continued instability.

Rather than let such a disquieting prospect weigh upon our future, how much wiser it would be for our governments and their populations to seek inspiration in the principles enunciated by the Court in order to promote here and now, with increased determination and speed, genuine reconciliation between the rest of Canada and Quebec within an improved federal system.

Goodbye to the Amending Formulas?

Donna Greschner

Donna Greschner teaches at the College of Law, University of Saskatchewan. This essay is abridged from the original, which appeared in Constitutional Forum constitutionnel *10 (1998): 19-25.*

Since 1982 Canadians have possessed a complex set of amending formulas in Part V of the *Constitution Act, 1982*. From its inception Part V has been afflicted with controversy. The Quebec government's refusal to formally approve the 1982 Act rests, in part, on its dismay about losing its veto on constitutional change. Amendments binding on more than one province have proven almost impossible, with only one relatively small change successfully overcoming the obstacles posed by the formulas. The rigidity stems partly from section 41, which requires all units of Confederation to agree to amendments pertaining to any one of several matters, including changes to Part V itself. The unanimity rule prevented adoption of the Meech Lake Accord. Moreover, several legislatures have supplemented Part V with statutory requirements to hold referendums on constitutional change. These statutory promises to facilitate direct democracy contributed to the demise of the Charlottetown Accord. More recently, Parliament has enacted restrictions on its power to initiate and approve constitutional change. The legal rules of amendment, both constitutional and statutory, have acquired such Byzantine dimensions that they seem designed to prevent amendments rather than permit them.

Against this backdrop of rigidity and failure, the Quebec Secession Reference presented the Court with its first opportunity in over
fifteen years to consider the critical process of constitutional amendment. Question 1 asked: "Under the Constitution of Canada, can the
National Assembly, legislature or government of Quebec effect the
secession of Quebec from Canada unilaterally?" The Court's response does not delve into the intricacies of Part V. Even though the
Court states that "[o]ur Constitution is primarily a written one" (para.
49), that "there are compelling reasons to insist upon the primacy of
our written constitution" (para. 53), and that constitutional texts
"have a primary place in determining constitutional rules" (para. 32),
it writes seventy paragraphs without any explicit reference to a specific written provision on constitutional amendment. Instead, the
Court emphasizes constitutional principles. It describes four foundational principles that underlie constitutional rules and practice: federalism, democracy, constitutionalism and the rule of law, and the
protection of minorities. These principles generate legal duties for
the parties to Confederation.

The proffered reason for the inclusion of principles and the emphasis placed on them is instructive. For the Court, the constitutional
framework must include principles because a written text cannot
provide for every situation that might arise in the future. "These
supporting principles and rules, which include constitutional conventions and the workings of Parliament, are a necessary part of our
Constitution because problems or situations may arise which are not
expressly dealt with by the text of the Constitution. In order to endure
over time, a constitution must contain a comprehensive set of rules
and principles which are capable of providing an exhaustive legal
framework for our system of government" (para. 32). This reason is
not self-evident. The application of unwritten principles is not essential for the stated purpose; it is not the only method of ensuring that
a constitution adapts to changing circumstances. The formal process
of constitutional amendment permits a constitution to keep up with
the times. A constitution with an unworkable amending formula will
require other methods of adjustment, however, such as the application of constitutional principles. By implication, the Court is faulting
Part V for not delivering the flexibility necessary to deal with new
problems and situations.

The Functions of Constitutional Principles

The Court assigns two functions to constitutional principles. First, they generate a duty to negotiate an amendment to permit lawful secession: "The federalism principle, in conjunction with the democratic principle, dictates that the clear repudiation of the existing constitutional order and the clear expression of the desire to pursue secession by the population of a province would give rise to a reciprocal obligation on all parties to Confederation to negotiate constitutional changes to respond to that desire" (para. 88). If the twofold trigger of a clear referendum question and a clear majority in favour of secession is met, then other parties to Confederation must come to the negotiating table. The Court notes that the *Constitution Act, 1982*, gives each party to Confederation the right to initiate constitutional change and that this right gives rise to a corresponding duty to engage in constitutional discussions (para. 69). Presumably the Court was referring to section 46(1), which states that the Senate or the House of Commons, or a legislative assembly, may initiate the amending process by passing a resolution. But it does not identify the provision. In any event, the constitutional text is a secondary source of the duty: "This duty is inherent in the democratic principle which is a fundamental predicate of our system of governance" (para. 69).... For whatever reason, the Court emphasizes principles as the source of the duty to negotiate. Part V is noticeable by its absence.

The second function of principles is to impose standards of conduct on the negotiating parties: "The conduct of the parties in such negotiations would be governed by the same constitutional principles which give rise to the duty" (para. 90). Principles will shape and assess every aspect of negotiations, from the agenda to the position of parties. For instance, the fourth principle, protection of minorities, will compel the parties to discuss various methods of ensuring protection for minority groups. The Court is clear that the duty to negotiate in a manner consistent with the principles is a legal obligation (paras. 98, 102). Therefore, it trumps the desire of political actors to follow the wishes of their voters.

Overall, the Court's description of the functions of principles and the duty to negotiate, when coupled with the absence of Part V in the reasoning, leads to the inference that in the secession context the strict application of Part V rules will give way to broader principles. The Court's message to political actors is that the written rules, and the rights of parties that flow from the rules, are not as important as underlying constitutional principles. The application of principles softens the existing amending rules, and thus fulfils their *raison d'être* of facilitating change.

The diminished importance of Part V makes sense in the context of secession. The amending procedures do not fit comfortably with secession because they were not designed for the purpose of creating two new countries. Consider the many questions about the application of Part V that would arise in secession negotiations. For instance, does Quebec count as one province for the seven required by the 7/50 provision (mandating the agreement of the federal government and seven provinces containing 50 per cent of Canada's population) in section 38? Until the secession amendment takes effect, it is still a province and legally must count in the formula. For Quebec to count under the 7/50 formula would mean that Ontario's consent would not be necessary. It seems inconsistent with the democratic principle that the most populous province should become bound by an agreement that Quebec is negotiating as a potential new state, not merely as a province. To count Quebec under the 7/50 formula does not make obvious sense. Moreover, at the moment that the secession agreement takes effect, the 7/50 formula would disappear.

Part V also presents difficulties with respect to delineating the negotiating parties for secession amendments. The Court assumes that the negotiating parties are the Confederation units who possess rights under section 46. Yet, throughout the negotiations, Quebec will be wearing two hats: one as a province and another as an emerging new country. At the same time, other provinces will act simultaneously in two roles: one as units of the old Canada, and another as units of a new Canada. Who will represent the rest of Canad (ROC) as a whole? The Part V formula does not give the responsibility to anybody. Can the federal government represent an entity which may be coming into being during the process of negotiation? Will it have the authority, or the inclination, to represent both the old Canada (with Quebec) and the new Canada (without Quebec)? These questions are fundamental and complex, and Part V has little to say about them. Nor, for that matter, does the Court say much about them.

One potentially pertinent question is whether principles are available "to trump" the written provisions, in order to resolve deadlock and permit orderly change after the referendum. We know principles can fill in the gaps between rules and structure the exercise of discretion bestowed by rules. Can constitutional principles also contradict or override the written rules of the Constitution? Overall, the message of the Court's opinion is that principles are more important than rules, notwithstanding the pronouncements about the primacy of the text (para. 53). The Court states that an agreement requires support from the "majority of Canadians as a whole, whatever that might mean" (para. 93) and that negotiation requires reconciliation of rights and obligations between "two legitimate majorities, namely the majority of the population of Quebec, and that of Canada as a whole" (para. 152). In an opinion obviously written with considerable care, these comments are not accidental. They may hint that the Court will dispense with Part V, especially the unanimity rule, if it stands in the way of peaceful transition. The Court deliberately does not address how secession could be achieved in a constitutional manner (para. 105). By emphasizing principles and assigning them legal force, the Court has given itself the tools to put principles first when they conflict with written rules....

The Road Ahead

Few people will disagree with the Court that negotiations after a referendum would be exceedingly difficult. Two different countries are being born: reconstituted Canada and Quebec. There would be two sets of negotiations, although likely not simultaneously. One set would negotiate the terms of secession with Quebec while the other would involve units of ROC negotiating the terms of their new arrangements. Both sets, especially the ROC one, would have numerous participating parties. The Court shows political realism in signalling that amending rules designed for a united Canada must soften during the emergence of two new countries. In February 1998, the *Toronto Star* reported the Attorney General of Canada, Anne McLellan, as having said that the "extraordinary nature" of secession would require one to determine "what process would be pursued at that point."[1] By stressing principles, and the legal obligations that flow from them in the face of Part V rights, the Court essentially has agreed with her.

Perhaps if a majority of Quebecers vote to leave Canada, political change will occur so quickly that the Court's opinion will play a minor role in the debates, deliberations and decisions necessitated by the rupture of Canada. However, between now and then, the opinion may influence debate amongst the political elite and the general public. Whether the opinion will reduce the likelihood of a Yes vote in a future Quebec referendum, and thus contribute positively to the federal Plan B strategy, is open to debate. For smaller provinces, one implication of the opinion is that they ought to begin preparing now for both sets of negotiations, as well as continuing with the Plan A strategy underway with the Social Union negotiations. In the secession context, their influence will depend on their persuasiveness, not on their legal rights under an almost-obsolete amending formula. And when power turns on persuasiveness, good preparation is essential.

Notes

Introduction

1. Kirk Makin, "Lamer worries about public backlash," *The Globe and Mail* (6 February 1999): A4.
2. Sean Fine, "Behind the scenes as history was made," *The Globe and Mail* (21 August 1998): A1 and A8.
3. *Bertrand v. Quebec (Procureur Général)* (1995) 127 Dominion Law Reports (4th) 408 (Quebec Superior Court).
4. *Bertrand v. Quebec (Attorney General)* (1996) 138 Dominion Law Reports (4th) 481.
5. Edison Steward, "New Hurdle for Quebec," *The Toronto Star* (16 February 1998): A1.
6. Stéphane Dion, "The Dynamic Secessions: Scenerios after a Pro-Separatist Vote in a Quebec Referendum," *Canadian Journal of Political Science* 28: (1995) 533–552.

Chapter 1

1. Jeremy Webber, "The Rule of Law Reconceived," in *Images: Multiculturalism on Two Sides of the Atlantic*, ed. Kalman Kulcsar and Denis Szabo (Budapest: Institute for Political Science of the Hungarian Academy of Science, 1996), 197.
2. Samuel V. LaSelva, *The Moral Foundations of Canadian Federalism: Paradoxes, Achievements and Tragedies of Nationhood* (Montreal: McGill-Queen's University Press, 1996), 3, 23–27.

Chapter 2

1. See for example, T. M. Franck et al., "L'intégrité territoriale du Québec dans hypothèse de l'accession à la souveraineté," in *Les attributs d'un Québec souverain: Exposés et études, Vol.1,* ed. Commission d'étude des questions afférentés à l'accession du Québec à la souveraineté (Quebec: National Assembly, 1992) 377 at 419-25; S. Williams, *International Legal Effects of Succession by Quebec* (Background Studies of the York University Constitutional Reform Project, Study No. 3) (North York, Ont.: York University Centre for Public Law and Public Policy, 1992); N. Finkelstein et al., "Does Quebec Have a Right to Secede at International Law?" (1995) 74 Can. Bar Rev. 225; J. Woehrling, "Les aspects juridiques d'une éventuelle sécession du Québec" (1995) 74 Can. Bar Rev. 293; J. Webber, "The Legality of a Unilateral Declaration of Independence under Canadian Law" (1997) 42 McGill L.J. 281.
2. J. Frémont and F. Boudreault, "Supraconstitutionnalité canadienne et sécession du Québec" (1997) 8 N.J.C.L. 163 at 203.
3. James Crawford, *Response to Expert Reports of the* Amicus Curiae, 12 January 1998, para. 17.

Chapter 3

1. Four aboriginal interveners made written submissions to the Court: The Grand Council of the Crees (Eeyou Estchee), the Makivik Corporation, the Kitigan Zibi Anishinabeg and the Chiefs of Ontario. The Mi'gmaq Nation was granted leave to intervene but did not file written submissions. In this article we will be relying primarily on the three facta of the Grand Council of the Crees. Although we do not in any way wish to diminish the importance of the other aboriginal interveners by describing the Crees as "leading" interveners, the Crees began formulating the aboriginal legal arguments in opposition to a unilateral secession of Quebec long before the Reference was announced and had published an extensive legal tract concerning the rights of the James Bay Crees and other aboriginal peoples in the event of Quebec secession in their book *Sovereign Injustice*.
2. Which include: *Charter of the United Nations*, arts. 1, 55; *International Covenant on Civil and Political Rights*, art. 1; *International Covenant on Economic, Social and Cultural Rights*, art. 1. The right to self-determination of aboriginal peoples is discussed in the Primary Cree Factum at paras. 73-99, the Reply Cree Factum at paras. 70-74, the Written Responses Cree Factum at paras. 29-32, and the Makivik Factum at paras. 79-99.
3. Factum of the Grand Council of the Crees (Eeyou Estchee) — Reply to Factum of *Amicus Curiae*, 19 Janurary 1998, para. 44
4. See N. Finkelstein and G. Veigh, *The Separation of Quebec and the Constitution of Canada* (North York, Ontario: York University Centre for Public Law and Public Policy, 1992), 25.

Chapter 7

1. *London Free Press* (27 September 1996).
2. Graham Fraser, "The Quebec Ruling: Canada Must Negotiate After a Yes Vote," *The Globe and Mail* (21 August 1998): A1.
3. See Bouchard in this volume.

Chapter 11

1. José Woehrling, "Ground Rules for the Next Referendum on Quebec's Sovereignty," *Canada Watch* 4/5 & 6 (August 1996): 89–97.

Chapter 12

1. Readers of John Ralston Saul will recognize this example of organic nationalism from *Reflections of a Siamese Twin: Canada at the End of the Twentieth Century* (Toronto: Viking, 1997).

Chapter 14

1. Graham Fraser, "The Quebec Ruling: Canada Must Negotiate after Yes Vote," *The Globe and Mail* (21 August 1998): A1.
2. Rhéal Séguin, "Federalist Cause 'Poisoned' by Ruling, Bouchard Says," *The Globe and Mail* (22 August 1998); Rhéal Séguin, "Bouchard Says Next Referendum Would Put Question More Clearly," *The Globe and Mail* (21 August 1998); and see Bouchard in this volume. Deputy Premier Bernard Landry and former Premier Jacques Parizeau shared Bouchard's enthusiasm for this aspect

of the Court's ruling. Rhéal Séguin, "Ruling Legitimizes Sovereignty Drive, PQ Leaders Says," *The Globe and Mail* (21 August 1998) for Landry; and Jacques Parizeau, "Lettre ouverte aux juges de la cour suprême," *Le Devoir* (3 September 1998) for Parizeau.

3. See Claude Ryan, "What if Quebecers Voted Clearly for Secession?" in this volume.

4. Terminology can be confusing when a country might break up. For the sake of clarity, I often use "old Canada" for the present reality and "new Canada" for the smaller, residual Canada that would survive should Quebec secede.

Chapter 16

1. Edison Stewart, "New Hurdle for Quebec," *The Toronto Star* (16 February 1998): A1.

Index

AGMV
MARQUIS
Québec, Canada
1999